Edward Everett Hale

G.T.T.; or, The wonderful adventures of a Pullman

Edward Everett Hale

G.T.T.; or, The wonderful adventures of a Pullman

ISBN/EAN: 9783743303317

Manufactured in Europe, USA, Canada, Australia, Japa

Cover: Foto ©ninafisch / pixelio.de

Manufactured and distributed by brebook publishing software (www.brebook.com)

Edward Everett Hale

G.T.T.; or, The wonderful adventures of a Pullman

TOWN AND COUNTRY SERIES.

G. T. T.;

OR,

THE WONDERFUL ADVENTURES OF A PULLMAN.

"It is a very good office one man does another, when he tells him the manner of his being pleased."
Sir Richard Steele.

G. T. T.;

OR,

THE WONDERFUL ADVENTURES OF A PULLMAN.

BY

EDWARD E. HALE.

———oo;u;oo———

BOSTON:
ROBERTS BROTHERS.
1877.

Copyright, 1877,
By ROBERTS BROTHERS.

PREFACE.

More than a generation ago, a common joke — one of the commonest — represented that when an insolvent debtor, or a rough who had been engaged in an "unpleasantness," or any other loafer who had changed his home, wished to leave warning behind him where he had gone, he chalked upon his door the letters

G. T. T.

These letters were in no sort mysterious. They meant and were understood to mean, "Gone to Texas."

Old enough to remember their use, when they were quite as intelligible as A.S.S. or LL.D., I have been amused and surprised to see that this generation does not know what they mean, and that a word of preface is needed to explain. I was so simple, and so far gone in years, that when I announced the title to this book I supposed all America would know, — all America would have known thirty years ago, — what these letters mean. I had no thought of a secret society or of other cabala.

For myself I had an early interest in Texas. The first pamphlet I ever published — and that, I see, was a generation ago — was an appeal to New England men and women to emigrate to Texas. It was printed in the month of March, 1845. I had heard at Washington, that winter, most of the great debates in which the annexation of Texas, and so much more of the later history of the country, were decided on. I returned to Massachusetts, convinced that the simplest solution of the southern question was in a vigorous and large emigration of northern men into that New Empire, to whose fortunes ours had been linked by the resolutions of annexation. And so I wrote and published the little pamphlet of which I speak, under the title " How to conquer Texas before Texas conquers us." It was an eager appeal for emigration. At that time I should have been glad to join any colony which would have tried that adventure.

But, so far as I learned, no other New Englander wanted to go. The great part of the only edition of my modest pamphlet remains unsold on my hands. The law, not then well understood, was yet true, — that freemen would not emigrate into a slave State, unless they had slaves to take with them. It was as true as was the other law that slave-holders would not emigrate into neutral territory. The emigration into Texas, never very rapid before the war, went on with all the difficulties which check emigration into regions which permit the institution of slavery.

The truth of the principle, that organized emigration is the best method, if indeed it is not the only method, by which an old community can direct the policy of a new State, was left to be verified in 1854 and 1855, by the organization of the Emigrant Aid Company, and the colonization of Kansas under the admirable lead of Mr. Eli Thayer. The great issue was then first made on a fair field, and the great battle was then first won. As an officer of that company, I had some correspondence with the German free-state men in Texas.

Having taken this sort of personal interest in Texas long ago, I had always hoped to see for myself the beauties of a region which all people unite in praising. By a queer accident, such as will happen even to writers who are "not too bold," it turned out, unexpectedly to me, that a hero of mine, named Philip Nolan, had a godfather of the same name, who really opened up Texas to American discovery and adventure in the year 1801. I gladly embraced a favorable opportunity to go in person, over the routes of his adventure there; and in this little story I have detailed some of the modest adventures of travellers in Texas in these later times. Let me hope that the little book may tempt some invalid to whom is recommended a milder winter than ours in Norumbega, to go to dear San Antonio, rather than to try the rough sea waves, — exile from country, — and the grausome horrors of a foreign language in Mentone or at Nice. Nor let any such unknown friend be deterred by the dangers which threatened Effie and Hester on the prairies. The railroad to San Antonio has been finished since they were there; and "beauty in distress," may now go from Halifax to "San Antone" without sullying a white satin slipper, if she pleases. Beauty in distress may recline on the sofas of a palace car all the way, nor leave one palace for another, but under the shelter of a station.

True, to do this, beauty in distress must not pass through Boston. There beauty would have to be transferred by cab or coach from station to station. If we found that necessary at Hearne or Hempstead, as it is not, we should say, "So much for barbarous Texas."

The emigration, which could not be hurried in 1845, is now pouring into Texas in an unexampled stream. The population doubles every five years. Why not? The climate is peerless. The soil seems inexhaustible; the policy of the State is such, that you have your farm for the asking. And slavery — the obstacle that stood in the way thirty years ago — is at an end for ever.

"Ten years hence, we will tell you who your President will be. You will not have to trouble yourselves then." This is the joking remark of intelligent Texan gentlemen now to northern travellers.

Why not? The population of Texas is now, at least, 1,600,000. If it is 3,000,000 in 1880, and 7,000,000 in 1887, will any combination of politics choose a President then whom Texas does not prefer?

Since these sheets began to pass the press, I have lighted on an old tract by Samuel Sewall (the judge of Whittier's poem, the same who hung the witches), written to prove, from the irrefragable evidence of the books of Daniel and the Revelation, that in Texas, or, as he calls it, "the northern part of the province of Mexico," is the seat predestined of the "New Jerusalem," — the site of the city which was to descend from heaven.

Columbus expected to find it, where modern research found Pitcairn's Island, at the antipodes of the old Jerusalem. *Quien sabe?*

There are who say that we carry heaven with us, and I believe them. If so, dear reader, may you and I find old Sewall's prophecy good, when next we take a Pullman palace, and

G. T. T.

EDWARD E. HALE.

IN THE PALACE "PITTSFIELD,"
   Lake Shore Railroad,
      Near Ashtabula Bridge,
  June 17, ST. BOTOLPH'S DAY, 1877.

G. T. T.;

OR,

THE WONDERFUL ADVENTURES OF A PULLMAN.

CHAPTER I.

"LOWER six," said the clerk.

"But I want the whole section."

"Then you can have all six; or, if you please, all of seven."

"Six is very well; how much?" said she.

This little dialogue passed at the window of the Palace Car Office at the Jersey side of the river, at the station of Tom Scott's railroad, which begins at Jersey City and from that point goes — everywhere.

She was Hester Sutphen, the heroine of this little story.

The clerk is not the hero. We shall never, never hear of him again unless we go somewhere by that route, and he says "Lower six" to us, as we will hope.

For, as all travellers know, six and seven are two of the best possible sections in a Pullman's

Palace. There is no difference between six and five if the even numbers are on one side and the odd on another. About other numbers you may be confused, but not about five, six, seven, and eight. They cannot be over the wheels, nor next the stove, nor next the door.

Now, if you are to live in a Palace, what right have you to ask any thing else than that you shall not be over the wheels, or next the stove, or near the door?

Certainly Hester Sutphen asked nothing else. She returned to her companion, Euphemia, told her that all was well, and, now that they were sure of that, they went to breakfast together. Although this story is written by the most faithful disciple of Jacob Abbott in the art of story-telling, the reader will not be informed of what the breakfast consisted. Other breakfasts, as well as dinners and suppers, will be described in their order. It is enough to say that they were in that admirable station house which Mr. Tom Scott, whoever he may be (I have not the slightest idea), or some subordinate of his, has erected on the Jersey side, to the delight of all New Englanders who travel, and to the equal disgust of the oyster dealers on the North River side of the city of New York. For the New Englanders who go West and South are now able to have a good breakfast and to engage good sleeping berths also, and the oystermen lose the opportunity, which they once had, of asking the travelling wise men from the East what are the relations between the true, the good, and the beautiful.

They went to breakfast (the girls—not the oystermen), then they took as interesting a walk as they could in Jersey City—which is not so very entertaining a place when you do not know where to go, and cross boys are just opening the shops—then they returned to the great waiting-room and bought a "Tribune" and looked at some Sisters of Charity.

They wanted to buy a "Herald," but were afraid this would not look reputable for lone ladies.

Then the great door opened, and they were permitted to go to their Palace. The Palace was named the "Golconda." They were the first inmates who that day entered its halls.

"Oh, my queen!" cried Hester. "You are at last in the Palace which is to be your home— who shall say how long? Here, great princess, is your throne," and she pointed to the eastern seat of Six. "Behold in me the humblest of your subjects."

"Well, dear subject," said Effie, laughing, "I

don't know how to act very well. Could you hang up this strap—and where in the world do you put your umbrella in a Palace?"

For Effie Abgar had never been in a Palace before. Hester, as you have seen, had more experience. Hester, indeed, was the experienced person of this party in American travel. For Hester had once gone from New Ipswich to Niagara Falls, and from Niagara Falls she had gone back to New Ipswich.

On this occasion Hester was on her way to San Antonio, in Texas, with the intention of opening there a school, or as the habit of that country calls it, an "Academy" for young ladies, if she found a good opening. If she did not find it, she proposed to look for another. For Hester was tired of stoves and furnaces, of coal bills and wood bills, of dirty hands and smoking chimneys, and the thousand other annoyances which wait on the latitude of forty-three on the Atlantic seaboard. And Hester was a born lover of flowers also. She had that "sixth sense,"—for a sixth sense it is,—by which some people love flowers for flowers' sake; not because they are pretty, or sweet to smell, or graceful, or suggestive, or objective, or subjective; nor because they are cheap; nor because they are the "fugitive poetry of nature"—nor for any other reason which can be assigned—but because they are flowers. And so it had happened that when in the autumn of the last year, after the armistice of a summer vacation, the battle of life began again for Hester Sutphen and she went loyally to her guns, she had said to herself—and in her journal she had written—reverently and carefully:

"As the Lord liveth—if mamma is well next spring, and George and Hattie, and the children—if all seems to be doing well here, I will GO TO TEXAS to prospect in the spring, and I will not spend the next winter here."

All this she had written with extra care in her diary—and it was all she did write that night. "Prospect" was her little joke. The next night she wrote, in a less formal hand, "Wrote to Effie to coax her to G. T. T. with me. If she will go it will be perfect."

And Effie had determined to go. She had no idea of staying there; but she was glad of the chance of the journey. Effie had been hard at work in her studio all the winter, drawing and painting—that was a joy and delight to her—and trying to teach other people to draw and paint—that was not so satisfactory. Effie was delighted at the prospect of beginning out-door work near two months earlier than would be possible in Boston latitudes. She arranged with the other teachers and with Philip — packed her charcoals and her tubes of colors — met Hester when the hour came, at the Providence station in Boston — and thus they came to be at Jersey City, as you have been told.

It is always interesting to be the first occupant of an empty Palace. I suppose Queen Victoria and Pope Pius and Dom Pedro have learned that. But many other people have learned it also, whose heads have never chafed under crowns. You sit in your Palace — how happy if you have "six" or "seven" to sit in! — and as these other people come in for a moment you imagine them to be subjects. While they are sitting down, they are, for their instant of discomfort, your inferiors. Then they rise to be your peers, as they also assume their thrones; and they, with you, examine the new subjects as they enter. Hester and Effie had not a large nor a very interesting troupe of fellow-travellers. There was a man with a sick wife; there were a few young men whom the experienced Hester pronounced to be "drummers;" there was an old gentleman who put himself in the wrong car, and had to be transferred to the Xenia as soon as the tickets were shown; and a few old ladies, who left at Trenton or other Jersey stations. "Rather a humdrum set," said Hester. But to both the girls it was all new; and both of them were ready, from every chance, to make an adventure for a novel.

I have called them "girls." Will they ever forgive me? But how can I call them "young women"? Did I not hold them both at the font in my arms?

They brought out their novels. Hester had "The Strange Adventures of a Phaeton," that charming story of Black's which lends its name to our little tale. If only "the mantel-piece of my predecessor would fall upon my head!" Effie had—no matter what. She read next to nothing. Her sketch book took her off from her reading. The droll old Jersey farmer asleep on his throne; the picturesque newsboys at Newark; the two stone posts of the college—is it a college?—at Brunswick;—just a hint of this and a hint of that, when the time would be up, and the train would dash away, and Effie had to take her chances of remembering the unfinished corners of her memory sketch. She took out her Prince's Patent Protean Pen—invaluable resource of the traveller. The blessing of a Palace on Tom Scott's roads, or Commodore Vanderbilt's, is that he who rides can not only read but write. And so Effie was able to write her first letter home. No! it is not worth while to copy it. Though, really, this story would be best written if I copied all of those two girls' letters; and I have a great mind to. I will give you just a scrap of this one, but I will not promise any more.

ON THE WING, March 28, '76.

DEAR OLD PHIL,—

. . . After eating our breakfast we went out to see the lions of Jersey City; and we found it a most interesting place. They have wooden awnings in front of the shops. We saw a whole calf in a butcher's shop, with his head and feet off, and his hair on — quite grisly to look at. Also we saw some Balm of Gilead trees. On the whole, it is a good deal like Chelsea. The country is charming as we ride. I like the Jersey flats near Newark, which make me think a little of the country Millet drew. The browns and yellows were interesting and relieved by a good deal of spring color as we came on. The wheat is coming up, and we have seen a little green grass, bright green in some places. The willows are coming on, and I do not doubt that we should have found flowers if we could have looked for them.

And so on.

The mailing of this letter gave rise to a little adventure. The drummers in the car somehow sat together,—a little further front than these two girls. As they sat, the high backs of their seats protected them in a measure from the view of people behind, and so it was that Hester could not see at all and Effie only see in part the profile of a young face turned away from the window and looking down on a book. Effie made Hester draw close to her, that she might see this finely chiselled profile and the pretty fall of the girl's eyelids as she read. Then she began speculating as to how they should get acquainted, how this poor girl could be rescued from that crowd of men who surrounded her. The gap through which they saw her closed up in a moment more, as one of the drummers put his hat on; so the girls could not see the pretty face any longer.

"Only it was not pretty," said Effie. "I never said it was pretty; I said it was fine."

"Fine or pretty, Effie, she must have a name all the same. I shall call her Fanny, Fanny MacPherson."

"Fanny fiddlestick! She shall be named Price, Fanny Price."

"As if we were at Mansfield Park indeed! She is not a Fanny Price at all. I will give up the Fanny, if you like, but never the MacPherson. Honora MacPherson. How will that do?"

At this moment there was a motion among the drummers. He who was nearest the passage, rose, stretched his arms and yawned, and took down his hat. Honora MacPherson did the same and took down hers, and, to the disgust of Effie and the delight of Hester, stepped out with his companion, a vigorous, well-formed man with an Ulster on. All that the girls had seen was the rather well-cut profile, and from that they had constructed their romance. As the day passed the company of the drummers diminished. One left the train at Easton, two at Philadelphia, and one somewhere else. Honora MacPherson and his companion in "eleven" remained however, with occasional absences in the smoking car.

When Effie's letter was finished, as they drew up at Lancaster, she walked forward to call the porter to ask him to post it. The porter was not in his place. She came back with it, meaning to look for him at the other end, when Honora MacPherson touched his hat and said,

"Shall I post your letter, madam?"

"If you will be so kind," said she.

And these were the first words they ever said to each other.

CHAPTER II.

THE two young men were named Haydock and Brinkerhoff.

Neither of them was named Honora MacPherson, nor had either of them ever known any one who was named Honora MacPherson.

It was Frederic Haydock who took Effie's letter and posted it. It is an open question, not yet decided by casuists or writers on etiquette, whether he had the right, or had not, to read the address; or whether, having the right, it would be quite gentlemanly for him to read it.

For the true gentleman is distinguished by his abating something from his right.

However this may be, Frederic Haydock did read the address, after he had run along the platform, and while he opened the box to post the letter.

When he returned to his seat, his friend Hiram said, "Who did your inamorata write to?"

"She wrote to Philip Abgar, 199 1-9th Tremont

Street, Boston. I suppose it is her husband," said Haydock.

The two young men were not accidental travelling companions. They were boy friends who had been parted for many years, had met by accident in New York, and had gladly stretched and squeezed their appointments a little that they might manage to start together on this journey. They had been fellow-students in Antioch College when they were fifteen years younger, when indeed they were scarcely more than boys. The college had been broken up by the war, and they had not seen each other again now for fifteen years. Well-nigh thirty years old, they ran against each other in Broadway. Whiskers, moustaches, Ulsters, look of care, change of expression, all were not enough for a disguise. They were boys still. They stopped as if it had all been a dream; as if there had been no Five Forks, and no Crook's Mills, no Battle of the Clouds, and no Beaufort; as if both of them had left recitations in physical geography yesterday, and as if they had happened to miss each other at prayers this morning.

"How are you, old fellow?"

"Hiram, how are you?"

These had been the salutations of recognition after fifteen years.

They were not both drummers, as the subtle Hester had fancied them. Only Hiram Brinkerhoff was a drummer. Nor would he have called himself by that name, though he had too much sense to resent it, were it applied good-naturedly. He was a travelling agent of a large house of druggists, and his district was south of the Ohio and west of the Mississippi. Haydock had been, since the war, the postmaster of St. Auguste in Louisiana. He had come home to Manitowoc this summer to visit his father and mother, and he took the occasion to come East as far as New York, which he had never seen.

It was of course that they should establish themselves at once at the same hotel; that they should spend every hour of the next week together, and then that they should so cut and carve their plans as to start on this journey at the same time.

Even after the journey had begun they were by no means talked dry. How had they missed each other, and how close were they to each other in the army? How near did the transport, in which Hiram was, pass to the camp of Fred's regiment! A thousand such matters as these kept starting up afresh, and each one, as it started, opened up a thousand more. They had of course to pass the time of day with their companions who were only starting on shorter expeditions; but, as these gentlemen dropped off one after another, the two young men found the afternoon devoted itself not so much to their novels or newspapers as to good steady talk, such as not even a week in the city had given them a chance for.

It is not to be pretended, however, that they were so much absorbed in each other, through the day's ride, as to be ignorant of the presence of two pleasing, pretty, and ladylike young women on the other side of the Palace, although "eleven" were in front of "six," as the "Golconda" was then running.

Honora MacPherson, alias Frederic Haydock, had caught sight of Mrs. Abgar's face before she caught sight of his. And it is very certain that he did not mistake her for a man when she mistook him for a woman. As he sat riding backward, he had better opportunities for studying the ladies' manner, without obtrusiveness, than had Hiram. Without thinking much of the ladies, they did from time to time confide to each other their observations, and, in the bungling style of men, gradually created a theory which accounted for the existence of the other couple, much as Hester had done, though not, perhaps, so accurately.

"Times have changed indeed," said Hiram, as the tireless train at last paused — so a fish-hawk rests before pouncing for his food — just as they swept into Lancaster. "I remember this place when the one horse, one track, branched off from the State Road to take us to Harrisburg; when a long bench to step upon seemed to be the only 'depot' convenience. My father used to tell of a woman who sold crullers, pretzels, and apples on a table on the south side of the track, who was so beautiful that all the passengers clustered on that side to see her."

Saying this, Hiram looked out of the Palace, and Frederic as well; but there was no Hermione, — daughter of that remembered Helen, there. It was as Fred turned back from looking for her that Effie gave to him her letter.

Anybody who has never seen other farms than Effie and Hester had seen in Massachusetts finds a thousand wonderful sights in the large-scale farming of Pennsylvania: barns more stately than churches, and fields without fences and without woods just growing green as the wheat starts, or just growing white as a snow flurry falls. The girls were at their window studying

Pennsylvania agriculture a great deal of the afternoon. The men had seen a great deal of large-scale farming. They had little to see, but much to talk of. An hour passed before either party knew it, and the train swept into Harrisburg to the surprise of all — when, of a sudden, martial music welcomed them:

"See! the conquering hero comes!"

"A little surprise I arranged for you," said Brinkerhoff to Haydock.

"O my queen!" said Hester, at the same moment, "as you first place your royal foot upon the ground, you see that your lieges are assembled to do you honor."

"Are we to get out?" asked Effie.

"Your majesty should say 'are we to alight?'" replied Hester. "In the first place, queens always alight; in the second place, the word 'get' is gradually getting itself banished from all respectable seminaries and other institutions of learning. And your majesty will perhaps regard yourself as under my instruction for this journey for the correction of your majesty's cacology. To answer your majesty's question, I think we will get out, and spend our twenty-five minutes in examining the institutions of the capital of Pennsylvania."

So they "alighted." There was no friendly porter to help, the other passengers were all gone ; and, rather to their dismay, the girls found that they had jumped down upon a snow-bound platform into the midst of a military band, a company of soldiers, and a body of men with badges, who were stepping forth and back, as sundry wellmeaning marshals bade them, whose own ideas were a little indefinite. True, they all meant to be eventually collectors of customs or postmasters, as the result of that day's marshalling. But just how this particular procession was to be marshalled, in order that this result might be gained, no particular marshal knew.

Nor did Hester, the lady-chamberlain in the midst of them, know which way she was to marshal her queen.

At that moment the band close to her struck up

"March, march, Eskdale and Teviotsdale."

Hester was just in advance of Effie. She was mad with herself because she was confused. She was confused because she was mad. Mad and confused, she welcomed Fred Haydock as an angel of light when he touched his hat and said, "Let me show you the way, madam!" Indeed she could not be certain, afterwards, that for just an instant, as he led her between two very fussy marshals and separated two platoons of delegates for her, she could not be certain that, just for that instant, she did not take his arm.

And these were the first words he ever spoke to her!

An instant more, and all peril was over. The ladies were both in the dining-room, and some nice Pennsylvania girls were asking them if they would dine.

It had been very easy, in the retreat of the studio, to say they would eat sandwiches all the way till they came to Cincinnati. But with those nice white table-cloths, with spoons shining brighter than silver, with celery rising sea-green from the water, like Aphrodite herself, to allure them, with a certain feminine craving for Thea Bohea goading them on — who was Hester, who was Effie, that they should refuse?

"Have we time enough?"

"Twenty-five minutes, madam. Rather more to-day because of the delegates, madam. Soup, madam? No? Fish? Troutfreshcodsaltcodfresh mackerelsaltmackerelroastbeefboiledbeef roastmu ttonboiledmutton roastturkeyboiledturkeyboiledh amplainsausageBolognasausagecoldtongue?"

Effie was aghast. But her lady-chamberlain

selected for her, and in a few minutes they were well engaged. The "pretty waiter girls" had provided for them both, when the hospitable chief of staff came to the table leading two gentlemen who did not seem to be delegates, to whom he gave vacant seats at the same table.

The ladies saw on the instant that the two gentlemen were the drummers of section Eleven.

Hester bowed and smiled.

Frederic explained, "My friend here was lost among the delegates. I believe if I had not rescued him he would have been marched to the State House to vote for Pennsylvania's favorite son."

Hiram tried to speak, laughed, choked himself with a fish-bone, and retired from the table coughing and with his face red.

He did not die suddenly, however, but reappeared in an instant.

Hester had not the slightest idea of entering into conversation with strangers. But she asked before she knew it, "Pray what is the band, — who are all these people?"

Then Frederic explained that the next day there was to be a convention to nominate delegates to Cincinnati; that these were the Eastern delegates attending this State convention, and that, as the badges in their hats showed, they were prepared to give the Presidency to Gov. Hartranft, Pennsylvania's favorite son.

"My dear," whispered Effie, "I am horribly ignorant. But I never heard of him before."

"Nor I, my dear; but we will be drawn by wild horses before we will confess it."

Then Hiram and Frederic began talking very pleasant and intelligible politics with each other, and they talked very well, conscious that two very pretty women were hearing them. The pretty women listened with all their ears,. but pretended not to, because they had not been introduced to these gentlemen. There was a little interruption when the waiter girls offered

"Plumpuddingindianpuddingricepuddingqueenspuddingpumpkinpieapplepiedamsonpiepeachpievanillaicecreamlemonicecream."

They all made their selections. But there was no more talk of politics. When the desserts were all secured, Hiram was telling a funny story of old Harris the ferryman, who determined a generation in advance that Harrisburg should be the capital of Pennsylvania.

Twenty-five minutes is a long time for dinner, when you think it is no time at all.

The fatal bell struck, the gentlemen led the

way to the "Golconda," the ladies took their hands as they stepped into the Palace, the bell struck again and they were under way.

A gray, grim sunset, but yet a sunset, on the other side the river, the river gray, and cold, and cross, then a little island white with snow, and bearded with birches, and willows, and balm of Gilead trees, — " Is this the Juniata yet ? " " I do not know." "This must be the Juniata." " No, this is the Susquehanna, still." " I do not know." " No — well — it makes no difference."

But the girls' doubts were solved at last, when in "eleven," with an exquisite tenor, one of the young men — they did not know which — broke out with:

> " Wild roved an Indian girl,
>   Bright Alfarata,
>   Where sweep the waters of
>   The blue Juniata.
>
> " Swift as an antelope
>   Through the forest going,
>   Loose were her jetty locks
>   In wavy tresses flowing."

And so on, and so on, in the verses of "The Blue Juniata," which all girls sang a generation ago, but which Young America has forgotten.

" Blue Juniata is yellow enough just now."

Then he stopped for a minute, and in a half

undertone in the darkness, said to his companion, "But for once that I have sung those words to this air, I have sung these a million times:

> "'Who is my darling girl —
> Chipper and cheery?
> Amy is my darling girl, —
> And Amy is my deary.'"

"You are as much in love with her as you used to be in Yellow Springs."

"As much! A hundred times more!"

A pity that so pretty a song as "Blue Juniata" should drift out of the memories of the young people of sixteen and seventeen years old. It is a pretty specimen of that school of song, which may be called the "American."

THE BLUE JUNIATA.

Wild roved an Indian girl,
  Bright Alfarata,
Where sweep the waters of
  The blue Juniata;
Swift as an antelope,
  Through the forest going,
Loose were her jetty locks
  In wavy tresses flowing.

Gay was the mountain song,
   Of bright Alfarata,
Where sweep the waters of
   The blue Juniata;
Strong and true my arrows are,
   In my painted quiver,
Swift goes my light canoe
   Adown the rapid river.

Bold is my warrior true,
   The love of Alfarata,
Proud waves his snowy plume
   Along the Juniata;
Soft and low he speaks to me,
   And then his war cry sounding,
Rings his voice in thunder loud
   From height to height resounding.

So sang the Indian girl,
   Bright Alfarata,
Where sweep the waters of
   The blue Juniata;
Fleeting years have borne away
   The voice of Alfarata,
Still sweeps the river on,
   The blue Juniata.

CHAPTER III.

IT is a pity, but so it is. If you choose to sleep in a Palace, you cannot see more than if you slept in a hovel.

And so our heroine and our heroine's friend climbed the Alleghanies, and slid down the Alleghanies, as if there were no Alleghanies at all. They came to Pittsburg, and they went from Pittsburg as if there were no Pittsburg at all. It was as if Braddock had never blundered, as if France had never conquered, as if Washington had never covered the retreat, as if Pitt had never become Chatham. No Pittsburg for our heroine and our heroine's friend!

Only the Palace rested a little from its bumping in the station at Pittsburg, and Hettie and Effie had a little quiet dream of heaven while it rested; and then, as it started again on its relentless course, they half waked, half slept, and dreamed of all the wretchednesses that their lives had ever known.

So they were whirled relentlessly across the "Pan Handle," by which domestic name that funny strip of West Virginia is known which shoots up like an inverted icicle between Pennsylvania and Ohio. So they crossed, half conscious and half unconscious, the Ohio River. But the longest night will end; and at last both girls had brushed their hair, and had otherwise adjusted their toilet, and found themselves looking out on the country, trying to make out in what Ohio differed from Pennsylvania, but a good deal puzzled in doing so by the "areas of snow," as Gen. Myers put it that day. For under snow all lands are much the same.

With all their pluck, also, the two girls felt wretchedly, and, if either of them had been comfortably alone, she would have been glad to cry. This had been actually Effie's first night in a Palace, and she had slept miserably. She even thought she had not slept at all. Hester's former experience had been not in vain. But she, also, had been bumped and tossed, and knew that the night had been the longest night but one she had ever known. That one was her first night in a Palace. What then had this night been to Effie?

Still, both the girls were brave. They had determined to go to Texas together in a Palace were there no other way. And neither would, at the first blush, confess to the other the misery she had undergone. Each, instructed by the other, tottered her shaky way to the washroom. Each was a little refreshed by the cold water. Each, before the wildly waving mirror, "did her hair." And so they sat together, as if no night of misery had intervened, in "lower six," and "lower six" made believe, in its silent hypocrisy, that it never was any thing but a large *tête à tête* sofa. As if they did not know, and it did not know, and all the porters and all the newspapers, that it was

"Two beds by night, a pair of seats by day."

Where they were, the girls could only guess by their watches, and by the "Traveller's Official Guide." They had been wise enough, not to be penny-wise, but to "buy the best." The porter was far too busy, in readjusting "seven" and "nine" and "thirteen," to tell them the names of stations. Indeed the girls were too much interested in his deft work, which they had watched with the sympathy of professional housekeepers, even to ask them. Effie twitted Hester that she did not know the names of the "creeks" and the villages as they passed them.

"What is the use of teaching so much comparative geography, my dear Hettie, if you cannot distinguish Coshocton from West Lafayette when you see it? For my part, I am only an artist. I am interested in the blue under the edge of that drift. But you, you are a school-mistress, and yet you cannot tell me when we come to Dresden."

No. Hester avowed in the secrecy of the Palace that she had never even heard of Dresden, of Frazeysburg, of Canesville, or of Coshocton. In each of these towns readers of this tale will follow her travels. How gladly would she have rested her weary head in one of them!

"But wisest Fate said, No!"

And they whirled on.

The girls learned afterwards from a friendly old lady of more experience to hide a Boston cracker under the pillow and to eat it before moving in the morning. But "wit comes afterwards," says the Yankee proverb, and so does wisdom. At Dresden Junction they were hardly settled enough to know any thing but that they were faint and wretched. It was an hour before the screaming wild beast which dragged them on was hungry again or thirsty. When they stopped at Newark to feed him, Effie looked out wistfully.

But the platform at Newark was snow-covered, and the porter was discouraging.

The girls doubted. Just then he whom they had called Honora MacPherson came up in the car. On a plate he bore a single mug of Newark coffee.

"Will you try a cup of coffee, ladies?" he said. "It is very poor coffee, but I believe it is better than nothing. You will have no other chance till we come to Columbus."

"Gentleman through and through"—this was the one thought of both the girls. Effie rallied first to speak, thanked him and took the cup. The mixture was not of that exquisite warm, reddish brown as delicious to artists as to epicures—it was of a hard, cold gray, with large black spots floating in it. But it was warm. There was a slight sense of stimulant in it, though the taste was vile; yet there was reason to believe that a part at least of the compound had drunk in the temper of a Brazilian sun. Effie despatched her half. Hettie did the same by hers, and looked for the porter. He was nowhere. But Honora MacPherson reappeared. Hester had her two nickels ready.

"Is that right?"

"Quite right," said he, and he smiled. So their acquaintance was advancing.

On the strength of those doubly-baked brown bread crusts mingled with charred Rio, and of a sandwich, a little dry, which emerged from the lunch basket, these two girls went to Columbus. Columbus himself, when, about half a league from the little seaport of Palos, standing at the door of the convent dedicated to Saint Mary:

> "He asked of the Porter
> A little Bread and Water
> For his Child,"

was not more glad to rest from his wanderings than were they. But it is not for this tale to describe in detail the white napkins, the brilliant spoons, the brown broiled chicken, the golden omelette, the rich gravy of the steak, the crisp crackle of the potato, the mosaic of the waffle or the ophir tone of the syrup, of the meal which lay before them. The people of Ohio have a proud proverb that "No man was ever hungry in Ohio." This may be true of men who reside there. Of these two girls, who had been shaken like obstinate medicine vials for seven hours and fifty minutes since they left Steubenville, one hundred and ninety-three miles behind, it was not true. They were so hungry that they did not know that they were hungry till the brown coffee stood before them, and then, at the suggestion of the warm milk and Alderney cream, blushed with that blush of a brunette in Seville which already a vain effort has been made to describe. As one of them is a heroine, and another a heroine's friend, it will not be well to tell what they ate and what they did not eat before they bade their hospitable host farewell and mounted the snowy steps of the "Golconda" once more.

"I am glad she is named the 'Golconda' and I am glad it snows. I feel as if I were going

> 'From Greenland's icy mountains
> To India's coral strand.'"

CHAPTER IV.

IT was nearly three in the afternoon before they came into Cincinnati. Effie thought they were underground; but this was her mistake, though it was dark in the station. The Southards, father and son, were there to meet them with their own carriage; and after a mysterious ride — all rides in a new city are mysterious — now up hill, and now by long level ways, but never down hill by any accident — they came to the exuberant welcome of the Southards' home. Fanny herself was at the door, unknown Southard boys helped with the straps and bags, and the two travel-worn girls were instantly at home. How like home it all was — and how unlike!

And when they were clean again, and all sat together at the early dinner which Fanny had ordered for them, she compelled them to open all their plans; and, in her turn, she opened hers. Soon it appeared that she had arranged for this and that and another excursion and enterprise, which would require six weeks' stay. On their part they had modestly prepared to go on the next morning. Against this all the hospitality of Ohio protested, and all the memories of New England; and it ended, as such discussions always end, in the girls agreeing to spend three days: item, the rest of this Tuesday, the whole of Wednesday, and as much of Thursday as would pass before they should take the "General Lytle" and go down to Louisville.

"I thought we were going all the way in a Palace," said Effie, not very sorry to be relieved.

"My dear Miss Effie," said John Southard, "do not you know that your own Mr. Everett said that one of our steamers is a palace above and a warehouse below?"

Effie did not know it, but it was not the last time that she found out that she was to be made responsible for all the wit and all the wisdom, as well as for all the folly and all the forgetfulness, of all New Englanders.

"You are but a feeble folk," said John Southard, "and we cannot pretend to distinguish between you. Do not be surprised if I call you Miss Marshall."

Effie did not push the conversation. But afterward she asked Mrs. Southard who Miss Marshall was.

"My dear, she was the most beautiful woman, and the loveliest too, who ever was seen since Helen."

So Effie found she was in high favor with John Southard.

Nobody in Cincinnati remembered the time when at ten o'clock in the morning he had been seen outside his own office or one of the Courts of Ohio. But on the Wednesday of the visit he sat on the front seat of his carriage at that hour, twirling his whip, and waiting — only thirty seconds — for his wife and the two girls, that he might drive them out of town on a visit to a friend of his who lived in a real palace.

"Not one of your Yankee catacombs on wheels, Miss Effie," he said. And up and up — still up and up — the stout bays pulled the carriage, with the laughing group, till they came into the open country, and then by pleasant roads through a cheerful region they came to the palace which was promised. The grounds delighted Hester with such evergreens as she had never seen or hoped to see.

"If only you could see this place in the end of May," said Fanny Southard.

"I am very well satisfied as it is," said Hester.

"I never was in such grandeur in my life," said

Hester when the day was done. "Yet I believe we were all born to such beautiful things; and I am sure I was more at ease than I am when Effie has made me climb up into her attic in the top of No. 99 Oswego street." For all this, I think Hester's wonder at the palace was, first and last, that the hall of the house was so comfortable as well as so fine. It is long, long ago that the entry of a New England house ceased to be comfortable. People make them smaller and smaller. They let the boys leave their dirty boots there. The stairs are ugly. People even fail to warm the "entry." At last it has not a chair, a sofa, or a picture. It is nothing but an "entry," a place to come in by and to go out by; and you are glad to be done with it.

But here was indeed a hall, — beautiful beyond any room Hester had ever seen, — adorned with curious and precious works of art, such as she could not bear to pass by, and, withal, the cordial welcome of the most courteous of hosts, who had, it seemed, stayed at home because his friend Southard was going to bring some friends. He excused his wife, whom the ladies would see afterwards. His courtesies were perfect; and in the glories of the palace Effie and Hester were at once at ease. Fanny Southard was all delight.

She knew especially, how Effie would enjoy the marvels of modern painting with which that house is filled — as perhaps no other house in America is. How often had she said, "If only Effie could go there." And now Effie was here.

When the ladies had laid off their furs and wraps their host led them into a beautiful drawing-room, which is in fact a picture-gallery. Before they sat down, or before Effie could cross to see what stood on an easel, he asked leave to present two friends who had called just before. These gentlemen were standing.

"Let me present Mr. Brinkerhoff and Mr. Haydock!"

The girls looked up and gave their hands frankly, with smile and laughter.

"Why, you are old friends?" asked their host.

"We have travelled several hundred miles together."

Then there was a little explanation; and in groups, or in couples, as accident, fancy, or courtesy suggested, they turned to what, for many, many days, must be the dominant temptation to any one visiting in that beautiful house — the study of its beautiful pictures.

"You are an artist," said Hiram Brinkerhoff to Mrs. Abgar, as she stood silently before a picture of Rousseau's.

"When I see what these men have done, I do not dare to say so. But there are artists of all grades. Yes, I am an artist."

"And you believe in these Frenchmen?"

Effie roused herself to a great struggle. Here was one more man who supposed that the French school of to-day is a horde of Bohemians eager to paint naked women; and she must pretend to talk with this man about things of which he knew nothing. Ah! well. The truth is the truth, and Effie steeled herself to misery even in these exquisite surroundings.

"I believe in such work as this. I believe in such a picture as that" — and she pointed to a country scene by Millet, while for very sympathy her eyes were brimming over. "I believe in such landscape as that of Dupré's. I should think anybody might believe in a picture like that gleaner," and she pointed to one of Jules Bréton's paintings. Then, as she looked almost indignant into his face, she saw how entirely she had his sympathy — that she need not have strained herself up to conflict — and she fairly apologized for her zeal.

"I think I know your feeling," said he. "My question was absurd. People talk now of French artists exactly as the English talk of American dialect, as if I spoke Texan, or could; or as if a Carolinian could speak Yankee."

"Do not let us remember them," said Effie, hastily; "only let us enjoy while we can. They will want to take us out of this room before I am in the least ready to go."

Ah, me! That is the difficulty in this palace, even with all the courtesy of its host. It is not a place for one day's visit, and, whichever room you are in, you cannot bear to go from it to the next.

"Talk of palaces," said Mr. Brinkerhoff to Effie, when he found she had never been in Europe, "they drag you to many and many a palace there, bigger than this, and with acres of pictures on the walls. But if you will trust my little experience, you will say that there are very few houses in this world, call them what you please, where is so much that you are glad to see, while you are not fretted with annoyances — where there is really nothing to be explained away."

Their host had at this moment taken Hester into another room, and they could speak aloud of him.

"You see," said Brinkerhoff, "that he has bought what he liked, and he has not bought what he did not like. I should be amused to see one of the professed picture dealers of Paris, or of Munich, or of Antwerp, try to sell him a picture that he did not choose to buy. It is not a gallery made to please other people, I should say, but to please him who bought it."

But Effie was not listening. In a minute she roused enough to know that he had been talking.

"I beg your pardon. But stand where I stand, and look."

It was Couture's picture of a boy blowing bubbles, when, perhaps — who shall say? — he should have been learning his lesson. Should he? Then we should have had no picture. He is not a thoughtless, lazy boy. He has a delicate, pensive face — more a girl's than a boy's; he wears a dark dress and leans his head back on his chair as he watches the bubble. His slate is lying on his knees, and beyond is a table with school-books. "Tell me that that picture will not be precious as long as there are boys and bubbles, mothers and sisters and slates and pencils! Who cares for schools of artists, and all the stuff they write in the papers about motives and tones and earnestness and fiddlesticks — when there are pictures like that — and that — and that — and that?" And as she spoke, she turned on her feet, and faced successively every side of the room.

A happy, happy morning was it. Marvel upon marvel in the house. How Hester's eyes opened when they came to rest in the library. The first folio Shakespeare, had she not seen that? The earliest Milton — was she curious about early books — or would she not like —— —— and so on, and so on. Where would she ever stop, if she began to look at these wonders? And then, the whole room, in the midst of what she knew were almost priceless treasures, was so comfortable, the fire so cheerful, and all the chances for work so convenient!

And then there must be a little lunch; and then they must go to the other library, which, strange to say, was over the stable — only the stable was a palace in its way — and wonders never ceased till they bade their kind host good-by.

They had to bid Hiram and Fred good-by also. But it may well be guessed that after a day like that, they could hardly believe that they had been strangers only sixty hours before.

CHAPTER V.

IN the afternoon of the next day Frederic Haydock was sitting, smoking, in the pilot-house of the "General Lytle" as she lay at the shore at Cincinnati taking on freight for Louisville. The proceedings on shore were entertaining — many of them new to him — and his position, screened from the wind by the glass wall of the pilot-house, was not uncomfortable.

His companion joined him, pausing a minute on the step-ladder which leads to the pilot-house from the roof of the Texas.

The Texas is the third story, so to speak, of a river boat, the story in which the officers live. Ordinary passengers have nothing to do with it but to mount to its top, over which they walk to the pilot-house.

To travellers to whom all is new, the pilot-house is on many accounts the pleasantest part of the boat while they are taking observations.

"It is nothing," said Hiram Brinkerhoff, as he

entered. "But I am never tired of studying the movements of these river crafts and their crews."

"They are so unlike the rest of the world that they have a separate column in the newspapers for their *bon-mots* and other small talk."

"You know Mark Twain won his name here. '*Mark twain!*' is one of the cries of a man sounding, as he reports to the pilot. If all river men were as funny as he is, it would be worth while to give them a column."

"It is much more entertaining now than the Court Circular is, though not in quite such stately English. But it always reminds me of the Court Circular, seeing these people are our sovereigns for the time."

"For that matter you might say that the children are sovereigns. I see that they have a column in these newspapers, too."

"Yes. Have you studied to-day's?" And he read from that day's daily this specimen from the " Children's Column :"

"DEAR SIR, — My duck has seven eggs, and I hope she will have four more. I read your paper every day, and like it much. I am eleven years and four months old and vote for Hayes. Truly yours, Abraham Lincoln Watts, *South Utopia*, Ohio."

"Who is Hayes? I see he is the 'favorite son' here."

"Yes, of that there is no doubt. He is the same man that beat Allen on the hard money question last year. Evidently a strong man. Did not you hear what that Mr. Southard said of him?"

"At the picture gallery? Your inamorata's friend?"

"I thought," said Hiram, laughing, "that the other was my inamorata. Or have you given that up since she proved to be a married woman? Yes, that is the man. Evidently a man of mark here, leading counsel and all that. We were speaking of the Ohio State Convention, and of its nomination of Hayes, and I said, rather too flippantly as it proved, that 'favorite sons' seemed to be coming to the front. This gentleman replied very earnestly that the country would be fortunate if it had any man of half Governor Hayes's worth at its head. He has certainly made a mark here. Surely you remember his canvass for governor."

"My dear fellow," said Haydock, "of course I do. But when you have lived in St. Auguste eleven years, as I hope you may; when you have tried to keep the peace between two thousand crazy and ignorant field hands and two hundred crazy and irritated Acadian Frenchmen, you will find that all your interest in questions of greenbacks, even of tariffs, even of sutlerships, is much less than your interest about some of the very fundamentals of government. Why, Hiram, in that little parish there have been seventy murders in ten years!"

But here politics were cut off as the engine screamed its last call to the loiterers, the bell rang convulsively, the orange-women, the banana-men, the candy-girls, the newsboys were tumbled on shore, a "gentlemanly clerk," with his hands full of papers, left last of all, and then an energetic, anxious, long-suffering mate exhorted a horde of laughing, careless, limp negroes, tumbling over each other's heels, to be lively and not to go to sleep as they hauled up from the strand that mysterious landing-plank which seems like an elephant's trunk, and the boat wriggled out from her berth into the current of the Ohio.

And so they swept down the river. The "General Lytle" got under full headway, and the young men sat till the supper-bell rang, watching the disappearance of the smoky city and the waning light of the sunset, made perhaps even more glorious by the smoke. A waiter came up to summon them to tea, and Haydock threw away his cigar. Both of them vanished into their staterooms for a minute's toilette, and when they were led to their table by the steward in attendance they found their chairs tipped forward, one opposite and one next to Hester Sutphen!

Mrs. Abgar sat at the end of the table next to her friend.

Both gentlemen, with equal spirit, expressed their satisfaction with their good luck, and had, of course, no lack of subjects in going back over the experiences of the "Golconda," the palace on wheels, and of that other beautiful palace not on wheels, which they had seen in each other's company. Of course it soon appeared that the ladies had never crossed the Alleghanies before, and were wholly ignorant of the ways and means, the etiquettes, luxuries, and discomforts of a Western steamboat.

One of them cited the expression which she had heard a day or two before — "A palace above and a warehouse below."

"Then this is our third Palace since we started," said Hiram, laughing. "That is doing well for Republicans in one week."

"As of course we all live at home in log cabins or in the attics of tenement houses," said

Hester, "we must be grateful for this infusion of palatial experience. Do they really burn kerosene in kings' houses, Mr. Brinkerhoff?"

Then the incautious school-mistress was provoked with herself that she had let Mr. Brinkerhoff know that Effie Abgar had told her what he had said in the picture-gallery. In fact each one of the four persons marked 'this point silently.

"As to that, I think they would be glad to. To tell the whole truth, the kings and emperors never asked me much to their evening parties. But I am afraid they are still under the delusion of wax candles."

"You remember one Palace that was lighted with petroleum?" said Effie.

Hiram laughed, and quoted:

"—— Many a row
Of starry lamps and blazing cressets, fed
With naphtha and asphaltus, yielded light
As from a sky."

"Yes, indeed; but, somehow, I have always imagined it rather smoky down there, have not you?"

"That was in Pandemonium, was it not? That was before General Rosecranz taught people how to tame the naphtha."

"Was it he?"

"I believe it was he."

"I really think," said Effie, "that Mulciber or Baal, or some of them, ought to have known that before General Rosecranz came."

"The children of this world proved to be children of light that time," said Hester. "Anyway, this makes a brilliant supper-room for us."

"And it will be a brilliant drawing-room, and, if there is a fiddle on board, it will be a brilliant ball-room by and by; and if you are far-sighted, Miss Sutphen, you can see in the distant perspective that the preparations are going forward at the other end for euchre, so that it will be a card-room also."

"The truth is," said Frederic Haydock, "it is more like a baron's hall than it is like a modern palace. At the stern here the women reign supreme. Yonder, indeed, in the saloon, or whatever they call it, I may not enter, unless one of these ladies bid me. Then comes the piano. Then, where you see the captain, is the real head of the tables, and the head of the feast. By special privilege, because Mr. Brinkerhoff has every thing of the best always, and is a favorite with the 'gentlemanly clerk,' we are permitted to sit at this table with ladies. See, lower down beyond the middle distance, if you will permit me, Mrs. Abgar — see tables unenlightened and not favored, where sit only men."

"They are 'below the salt,'" said she, taking up his figure.

"In a sense, yes. But it is the land of equality, and they are fed quite as well as we are."

"Do you really mean," said she, "that there will be dancing by and by?"

"That depends. If those people yonder, at the captain's table, are two young men who have just married those two young women, and if those others are the bridesmaids and groomsmen, we shall certainly have dancing. If, on the other hand, they are delegates from the United Sandemanian Conference of Louisville to the United Sandemanian Conference of Cincinnati, we shall have psalmody. If, perhaps, they are the 'Grand Double Quartette of the Western Reserve,' or the 'Pittsburgian Choral Union,' on their way for what the newspapers call 'a musical campaign,' why that tall lady with black curls will be archly singing,

'If a body kiss a body going through the rye,'

before we are an hour older."

"Let us hope," said Hester, gravely, "that the next song may be the 'Blue Juniata,' by the distinguished *primo tenore assoluto* from the Grand Opera."

For Hester and Effie did not yet know which of the two gentlemen sang so wonderfully well. And so they did not know which of them was so dead in love with that unknown Amy, and yet they were "bound to know." But whether Hiram Brinkerhoff did not understand or did not care, or whether he would not understand or would not care, or whether Frederic Haydock were equally indifferent or equally skilful, neither of them colored or looked at the other. Only Hiram said, "Our chances are rather in Coronation and Peterborough, I fancy. But you ladies found out, long ago, what manner of people those were."

The description which Haydock had given of the various purposes to which sooner or later this long saloon would be devoted was no exaggeration. It looks more like a perspective view of the Thames Tunnel than any picture well known to most readers. After supper, at the suggestion of the gentlemen, the whole party walked quite forward to the other end of the hall. Persons sitting there had seemed dim and hazy even to Effie's far sight when they stood at the piano. They found, when they came there that on the right and left, in their little offices, were the clerk and captain and other managers; and the persons sitting round the stove there were, clearly enough, men on business errands, without children or ladies, who gravitated to this end as the family parties gravitated to the other. They made room for the ladies to pass, and then Hiram flung open a door that they might look out on the night, look down on the piled up stores of the "warehouse below," and might see the picturesque groups of the deck hands.

At other times in such scenes, Effie caught every opportunity she could, by the strong lights of the pine-knots at night or under the effects less sharp of day, to preserve in her sketch-book or on handy little bits of cigar box memorials of the attitudes or occupations of these men.

The walking and talking were suddenly interrupted. Quite without notice, a strange drumming was heard behind them, and a smiling and beaming negro at that moment touched Hester and said, —

"Please, mum, the Indians is dancing!"

"The what!" cried Haydock, not wholly pleased with the interruption.

Then it appeared that on board the boat was a

delegation of Chippeway or Ojibwa Indians, who were on a journey somewhere, after having visited Washington. It had been thought fit that they should follow the Father of Waters to the sea, — and so they were all on board the "Lytle." Dr. Summerfield, a minister on board, had prevailed on the agent and interpreter to bring them aft in the evening to give an exhibition of their singing and dancing in the saloon, and it was their drum which had interrupted Hester.

With Mr. Haydock, she followed the waiter back into the cabin.

The serious red-men were leaping gravely round one of their number, while yet others used the drum, and she-she-gwuns, or rattles.

Dr. Summerfield explained that this was a very grave and serious dance of mystery. It was in fact a sort of Eleusinian mystery, and would never have been performed in this assembly but that Dr. Summerfield was known as a religious man and the devoted friend of their race.

Hester and Fred came back just in time to hear, —

1. *Na ha, — Tau ne;*
   Na ha, — Tau ne;
   Ning o saw pau wabeno.

The dance proved interminably long, and the verses which Effie wrote down, are only taken at random from thirty or forty.

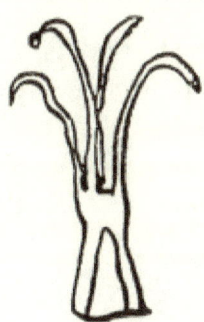

2. *Hi au ha*
   Ge he he
   He ge ge
   Hi au he
   Hi au ge
   We gau bo we aun.

3. A ne kuva
   Gi be aun
   Ge zhick — O wun.

4. Ke we tau — *ge zhick*
   Ka te kwa
   We teem aun.

The words printed in italics above, as the interpreter explained to her, are mere ejaculations, the same in English as in Chippeway.

The other words mean simply, —

1. "I am a friend of the Wabeno;" that is, I am in sympathy with this rite, and acknowledge my allegiance to the Wabeno who conducts it.
2. Here the Great Spirit himself, embodied in a tree, says "I (the tree) sound for my life as I stand."
3. The Worshipper says: "All round the circle of the sky, I hear the Spirit's voice."
4. The Great Spirit himself, as God of Thunder, says: "I sound all round the sky that they can hear me."

Effie asked the interpreter if he could not give to her the music. But he shrugged his shoulders, and, at the piano, intimated that if she would slowly and gravely thrum on any two keys which were not in absolute discord, with but the slightest remembrance of the time of the dance, her tune would be as good as theirs. But he wrote or drew for her, on the open page of her ready sketch-book, the pictorial representation of the words, which has been copied, with each verse, above.

The first is a necromancer's hand, in a supplicating posture, holding a bone, which is a charm or amulet.

The second is a symbol of the tree.

The third is the celestial hemisphere or sky, with the face of the Great Spirit looking over it. Within is a Manito's arm in supplication. On the right is a bird of good omen.

The fourth represents the beams of the Great Spirit all around the sky.

CHAPTER VI.

WHEN the girls woke in the morning each of them had the same start of surprise; for each wondered how things could be so still, and how she could have been sleeping so solidly. The slight tremor of the boat was hushed, and not even in her bed at home could either of them have enjoyed sleep less mixed with dreams than in this morning nap. In the earlier part of the night things had not seemed so smooth.

They were, in truth, now at Louisville; most of the passengers had landed, and the boat on their side was undisturbed by noise. When they were equipped to the last button, strap and keyhole, they did what Oriana or Darioleta would have called "essaying the adventure" of an interview with the clerk, to know how they should land their luggage and how they should find a cab or a coach.

They began together their walk down the long saloon. But, of course — as at the bottom of her heart each one had hoped, though neither had yet said so — before they had performed one-half of the "trivial dance" before them, Hiram Brinkerhoff and Frederic Haydock were seen approaching from the other end to meet them. If the ladies chose, they could suppose that the gentlemen had deferred their own landing until they could say good-by. If they did not choose they need not think so.

Anyway, the landing was featly and easily accomplished. Hester began by giving her pretty fur purse to Hiram that he might rightly fee the porters. And when both ladies were in the carriage, and he gave it back to her, he said, —

"I have paid for every thing. How long are you to remain here?"

"I wish I knew. Perhaps a day — perhaps a fortnight."

"I hope we may call," said Frederic.

"Certainly," said Effie Abgar. "Certainly," said Hester. "Good-by! Good-by!" And the carriage rolled away.

"It was really a piece of great good luck that we met them," said Effie. "They are thorough gentlemen, if they are drummers."

"They are not drummers!" cried Hester, really sharply — the first sharp words, however, which she had spoken on the journey.

Effie would not notice the tone. She only laughed and said, "Oh! I am really relieved. Not that I know what a drummer is. I only took the impression from something you dropped. But it is much nicer to have them fifers."

And by this time the storm was over, and they both laughed and rolled round in the carriage enough to kiss each other.

Louisville is a charming city, and charming people live there. And to young folks like these, fleeing from snow and ice and winter, it was pleasant to be greeted by spring violets and even Claytonias, and to see magnolia trees and grass that was fairly green. Of course they were told that the spring was exceptionally late and exceptionally cold. What spring, ever, was not exceptionally late and exceptionally cold? And they were very glad to find a good coke fire that cold morning at Mr. Sebastian's house. And the welcome, when the ladies came running down to meet them, was delicious. And this time Effie could administer of the sweets of hospitality to Hester. For the Sebastians were her friends; or, rather, they had been old friends of Mr. Abgar's. She had never seen them before, but, as Hester said to her when they were alone in their own room, it was as if they had known her all their lives.

So there was every sort of expedition arranged; every kind of pretty party — school-friends who turned up but had not forgotten — and, just as it had been at Cincinnati, the girls were made to feel that they had been idiots that they had not arranged to spend the whole month at Louisville. But, unexpectedly, on the second day only, came a letter which showed that if they meant to take the best boat at Memphis, and to take the chance of joining the party of Governor Champernoon and his family, they must not loiter long. After a very short visit, therefore, ten in the evening saw them bidding good-by to the Sebastians, and to quite a little circle of the Sebastians' friends, who seemed to Hettie and to Effie to be people they had known ever since they wore short frocks; though in fact they had never seen them before the "Gen. Lytle" stopped at Louisville that Friday morning. Lunches unnumbered; little baskets of Florida oranges; curious arrangements of cologne, — I know not what ingenious contrivances for Palace life — were forced upon them as they kissed good-by, and cried good-by, and shook hands good-by, and told good-by, and said good-by. Then the omnibus driver cried "All ready," and they plunged into the darkness and drove, through ways they had not known, to the distant station.

Mr. Edgar Sebastian made all easy there. "You had better take the berths at once," he said. "I ordered them this morning." And then to the porter, "Ready with your lantern, boy; what section has Mrs. Abgar?"

The porter looked, and said, "The ladies have number six."

"My dear," said Effie, "you shall have 'lower six.'"

"My dear Effie," said Hester, who was in advance in the darkness, and had come to the Palace, "it is our dear Golconda."

"It is the Golconda," cried Effie, as she mounted. And the well-pleased porter, glad that everybody else was glad, said, "Yes, ma'am. She had a hot box yesterday — was took off to cool, ma'am, and the 'Sybaris' took her place, ma'am. Glad you's pleased, ma'am. Six is all made up, ma'am." And then to Mr. Sebastian, "Will the ladies retire now?"

Yes — the ladies would retire. They bade Mr. Edgar good-by, and did retire. They had slept an hour quietly before the express came thundering in from Cincinnati, and it hardly waked them; and Effie's second night in a

Palace and Hester's third were such improvements on the uneasy rest of those not used to wearing crowns, that they swept through Kentucky all ignorant of Kentucky, and, by the time they had found their feet and their eyes in the morning, the train was running slow as they crossed the Cumberland River, in Tennessee.

"I owned to ignorance of Coshocton," said Hester, "but I had heard of the Cumberland River."

"So had I, who am no school-ma'am," said Effie. She did not say that as she and Hiram Brinkerhoff walked the deck on the "General Lytle," he had told her more than one story of his campaigning with the Army of the Cumberland. Why did not she? Because Hester had points enough for jokes already, and she did not choose to have Hiram Brinkerhoff called "the General." Besides, who knew? "Eight" and "ten" had their curtains drawn still, and so had half the sections on the other side. For all Euphemia Abgar knew, Mr. Brinkerhoff might be behind one of those screens of worsted damask next them.

So she only said "I am no school-ma'am." And then, when their toilet was made, they began watching with eager curiosity the peculiarities of

Southern life and of a Western forest, all wholly new to them. The open air aspect of every way station; the wholly new forms which loafing assumes in any strange region; the infinite variety and picturesqueness of the little darkies and of the big ones; the extravagant intricacy of the rags they wore; the queerness of the mules; the architecture of every thing, from a corn-barn up to a plantation house; then those strange one-rail fences to which horses were tied; and the multitude of saddle horses in every village, where at the North would have been wagons; it was all a curiosity. "Look here, do see this!" this was the chorus, and Effie's sketch book and pencil were in busy use, while Hester was provoked at the insufficiency of railroad botanizing. Would they never stop long enough for her to gather a handful of specimens!

The skilful novel-reader has foreseen that as, gradually, one and another pair of the damask curtains were pulled back, and one and another passenger swung himself out into the passage, with his coat on or without according as he were short or tall, one at least, perhaps both of the gentlemen who left New York in the "Golconda" appeared before the ladies who were their companions to Cincinnati. In this foresight, or shall we say in this conjecture, the skilful reader is entirely wrong. How can this writer say whether Mrs. Abgar or Miss Sutphen, as they saw the catacomb of the night gradually assume the aspect of a drawing-room by day, had any curious question whether they might recognize their travelling companions? Two German women with a little child, two Jews, an old man who seemed very sick, with a poor, pale wife taking care of him, and one or two very insignificant men, very tall and very thin, who might have been going to Memphis and St. Louis to buy or sell mules, or might have been agents of Brigham Young returning to report progress, but who carried 'no sign of what they were; these were the most of the passengers: — but an indifferent looking party, not encouraging to the student of romance. When "Fourteen" at last gave up its dead, the porter flew at the curtains and "redded" it with glad promptness, and then all parties felt that day had at last begun. The day was delightful. They could open their windows. And, without, the earlier trees and the first flowers gave token of spring.

"We are more than half way to San Antonio," said Hester, who had been ciphering and measuring over her Guide, "and I have not read three chapters in the 'Strange Adventures of a Phaeton.'" She took out from her bag that charming novel.

"Lucky for me," said Effie. "The minute you are well in, I may occupy myself till you are done."

"What a compliment! that William Black and my dearest friend should be balanced against each other, and that my dearest Effie should be the least bit jealous of William. I will not read one word of the 'Phaeton' till I see you deep in Racine."

For Effie had bought in Louisville a little second-hand copy of Racine's plays, which some school-girl who had "finished her education" had sold at a book shop for money with which to buy a quarter-pound of caramels.

"Poor dear Racine! To think of matching him against William Black. I will read you a little without opening the book."

So she repeated in the genuine French tragedy swing:

"Indeed — my dear girl — we shall come — to the river,
I know — that we go — for I feel — the floor quiver!
The man — by my side — has come in with a broom —
I must take — up my shawl — and must give him more room.

Hettie laughed. "Very well for a beginner.

But I — have I not heard the classes read Berenice or Athalie? I can give it to you with the epigrams. You should have an epigram at every second line. No great matter what they mean. How is this?

"The boy — who sells nuts — and is making that noise,
Forgets — oh, good heaven — that the nuts may sell boys!
Oh, my soul — is the word — of the angels above
That the angels below do not smile on his love!"

They both laughed, as people free from a winter's work will laugh at sheer nonsense in the exquisite freedom of a palace car. It shares with a steamship the luxury of having no door-bell and no postman. But in the steamship you are sea-sick all the time if you have any brains. In the palace car, unless you have been fool enough to travel on the short curves of the Baltimore and Ohio road, your brains are your own, and your stomach's lord sits lightly on his throne. It is the one place known to modern civilization where an honest man can be free from bores. A dishonest man earns the same privilege in the house of correction or the State prison.

"Hush! hush!" whispered Effie, as Hester ran on with her nonsense. And indeed the whole car was hushed, to listen to the weird strain with which a little German woman sang her baby to sleep. She had come into the Palace at Paris:

"Uf'm Berge da geht der Wind,
 Da wiegt die Maria ihr Kind.
  Mit ihrer schlohengelweissen Hand;
   Sie hat 'dazu auch kein Wiegenband.
'Ach! Joseph, lieber Joseph mein,
 Ach! hilf mir wiegen mein Knäbelein!'
'Wie kann ich dir denn dein Knäblein wieg'n?
 Ich kann ja kaum selber die Finger bieg'n.'
    'Schum, schei, schum, schei.'"

The girls listened with pleasure — everybody listened with pleasure. "Go on with your old novel," said Effie, "I will go and help her put her child to sleep."

And so she did; and then she had a long talk with the mother. And when she came back, an hour after, and Hester was willing to look up from the "Phaeton," Effie showed her this little version of the song;

> "Over the hills the tempests sweep,
> Mary rocks her boy to sleep;
> She rocks him with her snow-white hand,
> Because she has no cradle-band.
> 'Dear Joseph, Joseph, pray come here,
> And help me rock my baby dear.'
> 'And how can I your little baby tend?
> For you see I cannot my fingers bend.'
> 'Schum, schei, schum, schei.'"

Hester hummed it, and Effie hummed it. "I think 'schum, schei,' is excellently translated."

"So do I."

"What is a cradle-band?"

"Just what she could not tell me."

CHAPTER VII

"FATHER of Waters, indeed," said Hester, as they came to the Mississippi before they expected. It was not yet four o'clock, when the train was due at Memphis; but here were already waters "to right of them," waters "to left of them." How if the river should be in front of them also?

The truth was that the Father of Waters was on a rampage. He had come to meet them. It proved afterwards that he had never rampaged more boldly. And here were coves where had not often been coves — daughters or sons of his they were, according to Effie. People were going in tubs, on planks, and in canoes, from one cabin to another. Carts were standing up to the hubs of the wheels in water. All things brought back to Mrs. Abgar the delights of a freshet in her childhood; when, to say truth, she was captain of the fleet and led out the adventurous girls of Northampton upon the prohibited but too delightful excursions which they took upon boards or cellar doors.

Memphis itself, however, was not under water. Memphis is a city founded by General Jackson and two friends. At one time he owned half of the original town plot. President's Island still preserves his memory.

"If there are no pyramids yet, there are as good inundations as on the Nile," said Hester, as they adjusted themselves in a very long omnibus, which was to take them to the Peabody House.

"You will see a very interesting mound, madam, if you are curious in antiquities," said Dr. Summerfield their gray-haired friend,— so evidently a doctor of divinity and agent of the Southern Branch Publication Board of the United Presbyterian Church of the eleventh secession, that there could be no impropriety in his again addressing a traveller. Mrs. Abgar thanked him — and then, as before, he very kindly helped her in her curiosity about the Indians.

And at the Peabody House their hotel life with its intricacies and its solaces, began. Forlorn enough to retire from breakfast to a ghastly ladies' parlor, with horribly elegant mirrors in tarnished or burnished frames, with never a book except a directory from the town — or, by the kindness of the Bible Society, a Bible! But, on the contrary, a certain satisfaction, be it confessed, in the chances for silence if one wished to be silent; and for naps if one wished to nap unhelped and uncriticised. Of this independence be it observed, however, the charm was gone, for both these ladies, in about six hours after they had tried it.

The people in the house were as thoughtful and civil as if the travellers had been princesses. "See what it is," said Hester proudly, "to travel without escort." The "Chester Boone" might be there the next day at noon — probably not till night — nor must the ladies be surprised if she did not come in till morning of the next day. This was the report of the hotel clerk to them. Meanwhile would the ladies have a carriage? Or if they preferred to walk, the sunset from the bluff was a fine sight, and they would see the boats go off.

Hester thanked him, and when he was gone, explained to Effie that this meant that they were booked to stay in Memphis for eight-and-forty hours at least — that river boats never came as early as they said they should. "So now you may get out your colors, dear — you may paint my portrait, or that dear old black wash-woman's, or you may write a treatise on the antediluvian history of Tennessee."

In fact, the ladies wholly unpacked, took possession of the drawers of their bureaux, got out their books upon the tables, pinned up some of Effie's sketches on the doors, and gave their room a very habitable air.

They did take the sunset walk on the bluff. And for the first time they understood, or began to understand, what is the grandeur of the Mississippi. The western sky was all a blaze of crimson and gold. Low down — insignificant in every sense in comparison with those piles of gorgeous color above and with the rolling ocean below it — was the strip of western forest, all percolated with the risen flood, which makes what is called the western bank of the river. As if this river knew of banks or bars! That thread of woods — for it did not seem like a thread of land — was as nothing when measured against the piles of cloud above and the world of waters below. The girls themselves stood high above the flood, though the flood was higher, men said, than it had ever been before. What a flood! How angry! How sullen! How resistless!

"If a man fall in from one of the boats," said the Doctor of Divinity, who had joined them, "even his body is never found." Great tangles of floating trees were whirling round and round. Glassy patches, which seemed perfectly smooth, were bordered by ripples and even strips of rough waves, the glass reflecting the gold of the sunset or the blue of the upper sky, and the waves black and angry.

"Power — and wrath — and indifference!" said Effie.

"I never saw it before but at Niagara," said Hester, shuddering. "Father of Waters, indeed!"

What Mr. Alger calls the element of "human pathos" was not wanting in the majestic scene around the girls, and below them as they stood on the water-channelled bluff were thousands of people coming, going, or, like themselves, resting and looking on. How insignificant they all seemed in comparison with the flood! Was this perhaps a daily promenade of Memphis? Or was this an exceptional day? The ladies did not know. There was a circus in full blast on one side; below, on one of the steamboats, was a band of music. In the river — on their side of the river — forging through all the whirl and rush and eddy were little spiteful tugs dashing hither and thither, dragging great oblong barges of coal. Giant steamboats beginning to cough and puff and wheeze, and to give other signs of life were receiving their freight and passengers. Bells would ring, the band would play more vigorously than ever, drays, carts, and carriages would hurry, then the final words of land-lubbers, and at last the Elephant lifted his great trunk of a landing-plank, and the boat dashed out and away to be forgotten, while the wild raging indifferent river whirled and eddied on as if there had been no boat there. The whole was a most exciting and eventful scene.

The next morning, after a late breakfast, Effie did take out all her paints, set her palette nicely, broke to pieces a nice large cigar-box which the porter had found for her, and on its largest side had begun to try, "just to try," she said, some of the wonderful memories of the sunset, when there was a tap heard at the door.

"Come in!"

It was the clerk of the hotel. "I am sorry to tell you, ladies, that if you take the 'Chester Boone' you must leave at once. The water is so high that she is much earlier than we expected. They send us word that she has rounded the point, and that means she is at the landing by this time. She takes a little freight here, and will be off, they tell me, in half an hour."

"In half an hour! These trunks must be packed, this palette cleaned, nay, these dresses changed and these bills paid in half an hour!"

"I have ordered a carriage, madam," said the respectful clerk, "and it will be ready in ten minutes."

"In ten minutes!" screamed Hester as he left the room. Effie said nothing, but her brushes were already wrapped in paper, to be cleaned on board the boat, and the palette was in its tin case for travel!

CHAPTER VIII.

AND Effie never once reviled Hester, nor said, "It was you who said a river-boat is always behind time."

Ten minutes saw the carriage at the door. Ten minutes more saw the girls in the carriage. In ten minutes more they were in the "Chester Boone," had been introduced to her clerk by the young man whom the hotel clerk had sent with them, and this officer had said to them that they would be amused by the view from the pilot-house. He had explained, alas! that the Champernoons were not on board, after all! He had escorted them up to the lofty pilot-house, and there of course they found —

Not Frederic Haydock nor Hiram Brinkerhoff, but the Doctor of Divinity.

And he explained to them what they could never have known. "My dear," said Effie, in a half aside, "Do you see they are beginning the pyramids? Do you see those heaps of square stones half way up the bluff?"

In fact these solid heaps looked like causeways for giants where the giants preferred to have the stepping-stones square rather than hexagonal. They frowned down upon the waves of the freshet.

"Those cubical stones, madam," said the agent of the publishing board, "are paving stones. When the river goes down, the bank will be paved with them."

"Why, have they only just come?" said Effie.

"Oh no, indeed!" said he, laughing. "But they are too valuable to be swept down by the flood. They are taken up before it comes and stored there against the dry weather."

To this hour Effie does not know whether he was chaffing her. But he was not.

Both of them had their sketch-books out. It was all so fascinating. They never tired of the mules, they were so queer. Every black boy was more wildly picturesque, not to say mysterious, in his oddity than his predecessor. The "Chester Boone" did not quite keep to her promise of "half an hour," but in an hour from the time when Effie set her palette the "Chester Boone" and the travellers were under way.

And the kind Doctor of Divinity showed the ladies their first Indian mound.

Ah! if it were the duty of this writer only to make a little romance, in six parts, of the sail from Memphis to Helena! Material enough is there, though that romance should be the three orthodox volumes of Mr. Murray!

"But,"

as was before said,

"But wiser Fate says, No."

Unwritten be the history of that evening. Unwritten its songs, its theological conversations, its weird torchlight landings, the dance in the after cabin, the poker in the cabin before.

The next morning the ladies met by appointment, early, that they might have a walk on the forward deck upstairs before breakfast and see the sunrise. The sunrise was, of course, beautiful, but, as it happened, on this morning it had not the grandeur of the sunset. The morning was cold enough for them to want to walk briskly, and every thing was exciting and interesting. The "Tow-heads," as the queer tufts at the end of the cut-offs are called, the occasional passage of the boat through a cut-off, the tints of green beginning to appear on the shore, and once the salute of the "Montezuma," as they met her blithely working her way up the river — such things, all strange, kept them on the lookout. Then the profound solitude! That this giant ship which bore them should be forging on through this wilderness, where, but that they had seen the "Montezuma," there was no other sign of man. And she, she left only that faint shred of smoke on the air to show that she had lived.

"That smoke wraith represents history, dear Hester."

But just as Effie said this there was token of man's being again. A ting on the pilot's bell made them look up to him, and then they climbed to his friendly house to ask what manœuvre was in progress. He pointed far, far away, and compelled them to see a little speck which he said was a flag, a signal. So the great boat devoured the waters, made nothing of the miles between, and, before the ladies could believe it, was near enough to the rag or flag for them to see a man standing on the little strip of green which the pilot said was the levee. Water behind him, water before him. He looked like Campbell's last man, or like some Algonkin's first. It was he who had shown the flag.

The pilot explained that a road ran along the top of the levee where the country was not flooded, and by this road the man had come. In fact, after a few minutes, he pointed out the wagon which the man had left in the bush beyond.

Nearer the boat swept, and nearer. The figure of the man, his features, were perfectly plain. The boat touched, the gangway was lowered. Two black men ran down from the "Chester Boone" and seized the stranger's wallet and saddle-bags. He ran up the plank with them and the boat was off.

It was Frederic Haydock.

He hurried on board, and before his foot had well touched the deck the great gangway rose and pointed heavenward again. The pilot's bells struck "ting ting," the giant snorted his satisfaction, and the "Chester Boone" resumed her way through what was solitude again, now that she had absorbed this little atom of outside life.

Effie waited for an instant, just an instant, for Hester to speak first, as she almost always did.

But Hester did not speak first, and then Effie knew that there was such a secret between them as there had never been before. And she spoke first.

"I am so glad he has come," said she. "We did miss them all day yesterday, for all dear Dr. Summerfield."

By this time Hester was sure she could speak carelessly, and she said, "Yes, I am very glad he is here. But how in the world do you suppose it happens? And where is the other?"

"How does it happen, you goose? It happens that he knows who is on this boat. That is how it happens."

"Breakfast ready, miss," grinned and spoke the waiter from below. They hurried down stairs; and, as Effie had expected, but had not dared to say, next their seats they found a chair turned down by the waiter, as if reserved for a passenger delayed; and Dr. Summerfield's seat was changed. He was sitting on the opposite side of the table. Effie made the breakfast loiter as long as she could, from the beginning. But she need not have taken this trouble. Frederic Haydock's toilet was made, and well made, in five minutes. He came and shook hands, and sat down cheerily and freshly; and you would never guess that he had been all night riding across northern Mississippi in a planter's wagon, that he might strike the "Boone" as he had done.

"This time we did not expect you, Mr. Haydock," said Effie, merrily.

Hester Sutphen wondered if she were blushing. Why in the world need Effie have said that nonsense upstairs?

"I am amazed at my own success," said he, frankly. "The moment I found the 'Boone' was off, with you on board, I was determined that I would overhaul her somewhere."

"Good for you," would have been Effie's ejaculation had she been used to slang, even in its more gracious forms, and had she dared say what she thought. But she and Hester both silently respected the courage of the man.

And so a jolly breakfast follows. Haydock was courtesy itself to Dr. Summerfield. He made that nice old man find out that in taking care of these ladies he had won Mr. Frederic Haydock's abiding regard, if that were worth any thing. Haydock told, with great humor, the details of his adventures the day before — of how and when he learned that the ladies were in Memphis, and then how he took the afternoon train and pursued. He did not tell, nor did Hester guess, what Effie figured out from the guide-book afterwards — that his night-ride across those rough country roads was well-nigh forty miles long.

Then followed an ideal morning. Oh, thou hunted and baited child of civilization, think, if thou canst, what it would be to spend one morning of life without a bore, without a newspaper, without a mail, without a telegram, without a beggar, and without a morning call! Nay, think more than this! Think what it would be to have these evils wholly impossible to thee. Then imagine a bland April morning of the latitude of Mississippi — a new flora passing like a shifting panorama — shade if you wish shade, sun if you wish sun — imagine books, pencils, paints, papers, ink, canvas, a good piano, and dear friends — and then say whether life has a right to ask any thing more than it finds on such a morning on such a craft as the "Chester Boone"?

Dr. Summerfield asked Effie what was meant by "tone" in pictures.

Effie said if he would come out on the western guard — they called it "western" though it often looked north and south — she would show him Ruskin's experiment which illustrates his definition. And so before Dr. Summerfield knew it he and Effie were talking art, and he was watching her practice for three hours there.

And Frederick Haydock and Hester Sutphen were walking up and down the deck forward till she was tired. And then he had made for her a seat where there was no wind and just a little warmth from the chimney. And he was telling her first about old school life at Antioch; what a noble, unselfish creature Hiram Brinkerhoff was; what a loss it was to him to lose Hiram, and how happy they had been together. He told her of the war, how he had come down this very river with Sherman, told of adventures almost in sight of where the boat ran. Why! he came, nobody could tell how, to telling of his experiences in New Orleans since; what is the life of a lonely youngster there; where it touches other life and where it does not; how lonely it is, and what else it is!

And Frederic Haydock did not do all the talking. Hester Sutphen told him things, which she might have put in the newspaper, but which in truth she had never told to a human being. She told of her early life, of her mother's death, of Norton and the Wheaton Academy, and how strange it seemed to her when she was hardly seventeen to be managing for herself as a teacher of girls in the Southwest Milan Seminary. She fairly caught herself asking him, as if he had been Effie Abgar herself, if he thought she did wrong when she defied the secretary of the trustees at Southwest Milan.

And Frederic Haydock had to bite his tongue out lest he should say,

" You cannot do wrong. If you said it, it was right."

But he did not say that. Metaphorically he did bite his tongue out, and then with the new tongue, which came in the place of that bitten one, he said:

" I do not know what you call right. I know that I should have been much pleased with myself if I had been half so civil. And I am so glad you left the brutes, if you did leave them."

" Leave them! " said Hester. " I left that horrid place before night, and I hope I may never see it again. My dear Mr. Haydock, I did not know " —

But what she did not know Fred Haydock was not told. Just at that moment from the deck below, a clear tenor voice sang:

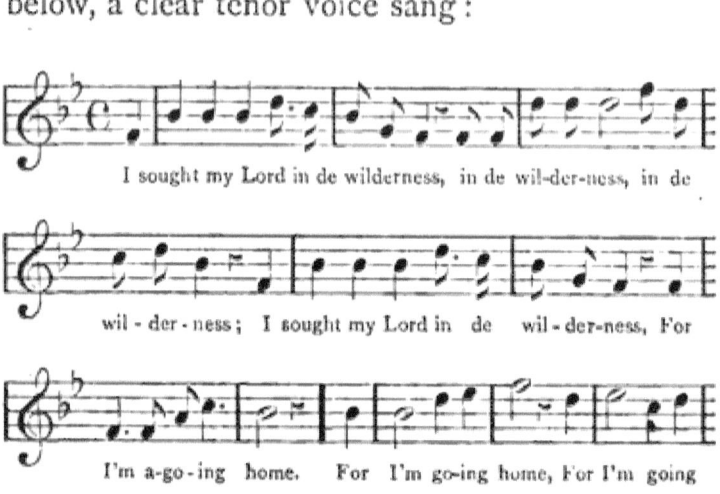

I sought my Lord in de wilderness, in de wil-der-ness, in de wil-der-ness; I sought my Lord in de wil-der-ness, For I'm a-go-ing home. For I'm go-ing home, For I'm going

home; I'm just git-ting read-y, For I'm go-ing home.

The wild, clear notes rang out so as to startle them both. Hester ran forward to look over the rail, and Haydock, without so much eagerness, followed. Neither he nor she knew that three hours had passed since breakfast.

The voice went on:

> I found free grace in de wilderness,
>   In de wilderness, in de wilderness;
> I found free grace in de wilderness,
>   For I'm a going home.
>   For I'm going home, for I'm going home;
> I'm just gitting ready, for I'm going home.

With the third verse some twenty of the deck hands took up the chorus:

> My father preaches in de wilderness,
>   In de wilderness, in de wilderness, —

And so the weird song went on; — and Mr. Haydock's *tête-à-tête* with Miss Sutphen was, for the moment, ended.

CHAPTER IX.

AS they went south the shores grew greener, and the air more soft. Once, as they ran in to the levee for some wood, Effie broke off with her own hand a branch of fresh leaves, quite large. Fred Haydock told her that she was the dove after the deluge. And after every meal, dinner, supper, breakfast — how few they were when one came to count them — it seemed more and more a thing of course that, while Effie painted on the after-guards, or wrote in the after-cabin, Mr. Haydock and Miss Sutphen should be sitting in some shelter forward, or that he should be reading to her the " Ring and the Book" while she knitted, or that they should be walking together for exercise, or in the evening, they should be singing together at the same piano. It was clear enough, however, the first time that Fred Haydock sang, that he was not the absolute tenor who had sung the praise of his own Amy in the dark Palace on the banks of the Juniata.

And all three of them — all four, if you count in Dr. Summerfield, who was very lovely and kind all the time — all four came to be good friends with the other cabin travellers. They had good novels which they read aloud in the ladies' end of the cabin. At night they had glees or psalmody. At the mouth of the Tennessee River the boat had taken on a very wild but very simple family, who had somehow heard of Texas and were going there, with the most pathetic ignorance as to what and where it was, and why they were going. But, from the old grandsire of eighty-five, who seemed for ever young when there was a question as to a new home, down to shy girls of four years and adventurous boys of six and seven, dressed in the most extraordinary costume which ever the wit of Northern Alabama devised, all were delighted to be on the move.

And to the magic of Effie's kindness this tall handsome girl, shy as the children, who for a day staid in her state-room she was so frightened, revealed herself as a bride. Never did the designer, in distant Lawrence, who painted the pattern for that calico, suppose it was to be worn as a bride's travelling dress! But no matter for that! As true a heart beat under it as ever beat under

Madame Demorest's regulation uniform, and she and he, so soon as they were married in the old home on the western slope of the Alleghanies back in Western Virginia, had determined to go to Florida. Why to Florida, even Effie, with all her tact, could not discover. She tried them with talk of oranges and sugar-cane and bananas. But they seemed to have little care for these things. Even Effie could not imagine that that stout young bridegroom had a hole in his lungs. No! It was only that they were determined that they would go somewhere and that they had heard of Florida.

"Like some other people I know," said Hester, meekly, "who might be sitting over a hard coal fire now, if they wanted to."

"Only they did not want to," said Mrs. Abgar, laughing. "Dear heart, it is the mania of the American people. They must 'pull up stakes' and travel."

"Say, rather," said Dr. Summerfield, more wisely, "it is the mania of that part of the American people whom you and I meet in steamboats. If we wanted to study the traits of those who stay at home we must knock at the doors of their homes to find them."

"That's true enough! I am as wise as the English travellers who think all Americans live in hotels, because those they see in hotels live in them. What can they think the houses they ride by are built for?"

They had poked their great nose upon the levee once and again, — now to leave a barrel, now, it would seem, only to leave a newspaper — perhaps to take an order — once to leave two bedsteads, a rocking-chair, a cooking-stove, a bride, her trunks and a bridegroom; in short, for any device by which civilization might be set forward in what seemed an utter wilderness. It was quite late in the afternoon that the clerk came aft for the purpose to say that they had some heavy boilers to land at Mr. Van Meter's plantation, and perhaps the ladies would like to walk.

Like to! — of course they did. They landed and were almost tempted to kneel like crusaders and kiss the sod, so delicious was it to find spring really in sway, — to gather a handful of even the simplest weeds. They struck off, up the river, on the levee for a long pull, assured that they might safely be gone an hour. But — shall it be confessed? — in ten minutes Hester was frightened. If the "Boone" should go with all their household goods, and they have to spend the rest of their lives in Mississippi! Dr. Summerfield tried to reassure her. But the pleasure of the walk was gone, and after pretending they were not afraid a little they turned back with one accord, built larger their branches of green leaves, and, like Birnam Wood indeed, approached the friendly monster.

It was impossible to believe that they had been only thirty hours on the boat. In that time they had entered on a wholly new arrangement of time and life. They had passed from coal fires to balmy spring weather and delicate green foliage; and also — ah me! — Hester Sutphen had held two long confidential talks with Fred Haydock. It seemed as if they had been a month on the voyage and the boat was home.

As they drew near the boat a gentleman came out from a little whitewashed shed which seemed to be an outlying building of the plantation, of which the larger buildings were hidden by trees, a quarter of a mile away. He took out money, which he gave to the black boy by his side, and then with rapid step advanced to the "Chester Boone," about a hundred yards in front of our party. The boy followed with his carpet-bag.

Frederic Haydock and Hester Sutphen were walking behind Dr. Summerfield and Mrs. Abgar, occupied with each other.

Effie had her eyes open. She suddenly made a horrible botch about something Dr. Summerfield was telling her, and said she was very glad Mr. Glass was deposed by his Presbytery, when she did not in the least know what she was saying. The truth was that she was simply watching the stranger and the black boy. At last she forced herself to turn back and say,

"Mr. Haydock, is not that your friend Mr. Brinkerhoff?"

Fred Haydock started, had the question repeated to him, looked forward and cried, "Of course," then with a queer school-boy war-whoop and three shrill calls, " Hi! hi! hi!" he brought the stranger to bay.

The moment Hiram Brinkerhoff turned he recognized them. A minute more and they were all together, and he was congratulating himself that he had not taken the "Morgan," as she passed down that very day.

To say the truth Effie Abgar was not very sorry. For she had felt already that the time might come when Dr. Summerfield should be perfectly informed as to tone, color, perspective, middle distance, foreground, broken lights, motive and action; and she was quite certain that she had herself received all she could digest as to the relations between the Directors of the Publishing Board and the Trustees, and about the legitimate supervision of the Board of Managers and the President on the affairs of both these bodies.

For Frederic Haydock and Hester Sutphen, they seemed to be in a mood in which most things were satisfactory. Both of them seemed to think it was quite as well that Hiram Brinkerhoff should be there. They would have thought it quite as well if he had not been there.

For Hiram Brinkerhoff himself, he expressed himself very promptly the moment they were all on board.

"It is so lucky that I struck you! Have you ever seen a sugar plantation, Mrs. Abgar?"

"Only in Vermont," said she. "We put on long boots, and then I filled mine with wet snow and retired ignominiously."

"Then you are just the person to see the finest plantation in the United States, and I believe in the world. If you count in the men and women who carry it on, you will say so too."

Fred Haydock and Miss Sutphen were by this time looking at something in his scrap-book, which he had brought out from his state-room.

"Miss Sutphen!" cried the impetuous Hiram,

eager in his plan, "let me interrupt you for a moment, for this must be settled before the boat starts. Would not you like to make a visit at the finest sugar plantation on the river? We could stop to-morrow night."

"What did you say?" said Hester, startled a little, and hardly getting her vessel into action.

"I want to persuade you ladies to stop at a beautiful plantation on the river and see the way people live here. Will you stay if Mrs. Abgar will?"

"Stay — where?" said Mrs. Abgar. "This is the first I have heard of it. You do not expect us to stay anywhere where we are not invited."

"No, indeed; but if you will only do it you will be invited in no time. This is the whole story,"— and Hiram had to speak fast, for the bell was beginning to ring the wandering passengers on board — "I am on my way down to this earthly paradise, a fine plantation on the coast. Mrs. Abgar, it is called Arcadie; is not that a pretty name? Mr. Le Clerc will be delighted if you will both make them a visit, and Madame Le Clerc and my lovely friend Eugenie and Miss Ferguson, they are all so nice. Now just say you could possibly stop there, and they would be so much pleased to see you." Then, as he saw his friend Fred's woe-begone face, Hiram added, "If you would all give up just two days to see this beautiful place, why you would enjoy it as much in one way as you did Cincinnati in another."

By this happy word "all" poor Fred was saved from the lowest depths. If he was not to be counted out from the party they might stay a month for all he cared.

But Mrs. Abgar was herself again. Without the least asperity, but with perfectly defined firmness, she said, "Oh think a moment, Mr. Brinkerhoff, and you see it is out of the question. How could Miss Sutphen and I think of pushing ourselves, never so indirectly, on people we had never seen?"

Hiram Brinkerhoff saw he had made a botch of it, and had sense enough not to persist in a blunder. He retired to arrange for his stateroom, and in a few minutes the boat was under way.

That evening Doctor Summerfield was able to prepare his quarterly report, without giving up his time to the instruction or entertainment of Mrs. Abgar. Mr. Hiram Brinkerhoff and she sat in the pilot-house, while Mr. Haydock and Miss Sutphen were well wrapped in travelling cloaks somewhere forward. Were they studying the newer stars which began to appear south of the sky lines more familiar to her? Were they discussing favorite novels? Was he telling her old stories of the camp, and she, to her own surprise, going over old hidden experiences of her own life which she had hardly entrusted even to Effie? Ah me! I cannot tell. Only it was a long eager talk, and neither of them knew how fast the time passed by.

For Mrs. Abgar, she was not sorry, as has been said, to have so intelligent a man to talk with. The pilot said but little, sometimes had a word for a young man by him, what Mark Twain calls a cub, — who regarded him with untold reverence, and seemed to be learning to pilot; and, when Effie or Hiram Brinkerhoff asked for any information, the pilot gave it cordially and intelligently. A monarch he, and a well-bred monarch, who knew his place. Mrs. Abgar was not more than woman. She was not, therefore, without curiosity to learn more about that Amy of whom he had sung with the exquisite tenor, and with whom he was more in love than ever, after fifteen years. Hiram Brinkerhoff was not a pennyweight more than man. He was, therefore, very curious to know more of the Philip

Abgar who was willing to let this beautiful wife travel without escort so far from home for so long a time. Why did she never drop a word about him? Perhaps Effie asked herself the question, "Why did he never drop a word about Amy?" But, when she made little plans of leading up to the unknown Amy, somehow she had not the courage to carry them out. And for him, in his blundering man-fashion, he took it for granted that something would reveal all mysteries about Philip Abgar, and so he made no plans at all. So the long evening sped by without any personal talk. But it were hard to tell what other subject, except these personal matters, was not talked upon. Art, criticism, literature, poetry, actors, actresses, artists of every kind, music and musicians, the opera and the great singers, magazines and publishers, the authors he had known and those she wanted to know, the books she had read and those of them which he knew and those he did not know, history, philosophy, theology, religion, hymns and hymn-writers, preachers and sermons, politics, politicians, race, beggars, social science, charity, housekeeping, party-giving, dancing, talking, friends, friendship, love, marriage, home, education, schools, public and private, governesses, only children, large families — what in the world does not come in review when a thoughtful, high-trained young man, who has lived much alone, has travelled much abroad and has read many books, happens to meet with a high-trained young woman, who has read many books, has lived much alone and has never gone abroad!

What interested Effie most, or what she thought interested her most, was that he had not only seen many States, but "many men." She remembered the classical lines. He had the most modest way of speaking of them, but he seemed to have had a gift of meeting just the interesting people. Thus, when they talked of style, she said, "General Grant's English is remarkably good. Did you happen to read his report of the very last battle of the war?"

"I was in Washington the day it was published. As it happened, I had met him only the night before, and it seemed as if he were talking."

Or, when something was said of the perspective of clouds, and she cited Ruskin, he said, "No man looks less like your idea of him. He came into the reading-room of the Workingmen's College, once when I was sitting there, and fell into talk with a gentleman by my side." He had seen Napoleon at his last review; he had heard Martineau preach; he was present when the Queen opened Parliament; he was on duty at Norfolk the day Jeff. Davis was imprisoned; he had in his trunk the photograph likeness which the President of Mexico had given him. All this came out by the merest accidents; nor was there the least wish on his part to say, "I was here," or "I was there." But, in three hours' talk, there were just enough of these accidents to surprise Effie with the thought of how very quiet her life had been — and how much it had been a life of books while his had been a life of action.

On his part there was not surprise that she knew so much, and had thought so much, and had felt so much. For Effie Abgar was not the first intelligent and charming woman whom Hiram Brinkerhoff had met in this active life. Perhaps there was no surprise at all. Perhaps, from the first, he took her even balance, what seemed to him the perfect harmony of her thoughts and her emotions, as something entirely of course in a woman whose voice was so sweet, whose face was so lovely, whose motion was so graceful, and whose bearing was so dignified and yet so easy. When he went to bed that night, and tried to analyze the delight of this long evening's talk, he did not own to surprise. He took it all as a thing of course that it should be delightful. What was unusual, he said to himself, was that she should be so thoroughly right, even on subjects where you would have said she might know nothing, and might never have thought. That with sense so acute, and passions so warm, she should never overstep by a hair's breadth; and that with judgment so steady, analysis so perfect, and conscience so stern, she should never be cold, nor fall short by a hand-breadth. Her choice of words was wonderful. Any fool could see that, he said to himself. But how in the world does she know things which nobody can have told her; pass correct judgment on the instant in cases which she has not heard argued; and, in short, without any experience of the world, more than rival in nicety of perception the oldest stager of them all?

All which, Master Hiram Brinkerhoff, is to ask why a truly noble woman is wholly outside and beyond the scales, and standards, and measuring staves of your human philosophies and analyses.

All four — they slept in their several state-rooms happily and soundly. It was only Dr. Summerfield, who sat up too late over his figures, and could not make the accounts balance, who lay tossing in bed regretting his third cup of green tea.

Our little story must not linger. Given two ladies who loved each other, and two men who loved each other, who had so fortunately and so skilfully gained together the luxurious repose and companionship of a first-class packet-boat on the river; it is not hard to imagine one part of what passed on the happy spring day which followed their meeting. For that varied adventure which relieves such a voyage of all monotony, the story must not pause to speak of it. Only, after dinner, after the ladies' naps, when they were all together in the pilot-house, a smoke miles below, far down beyond the green, announced an approaching vessel. Before the travellers could make out her form, the pilot had declared that she was the "River Queen" on her way up from New Orleans.

A mile in five minutes by one boat, and a mile in three minutes by the other, as they approach each other, bring the two soon together. Then signals by the bell intimated that the "Queen" wished to speak the "Boone;" the engines of each boat were "slowed," and they drew near each other cautiously. An instant more showed that no one was to cross from boat to boat as had been at first supposed. The first officer of the "Queen" showed himself on her Texas, and in his hand waved a paper parcel. As the boats passed he flung it with a skilful throw; one of the hands of the "Boone" caught it and tossed it to the waiting captain above. Both boats swept off on their course, whistled courteously a parting salute, and, as they say in the French chambers, "the incident was exhausted."

Not quite exhausted! In a moment more the captain came up into the pilot-house, a most unusual courtesy. He handed to Mrs. Abgar a letter.

"The 'Queen' stopped to leave this for you, Madame. Mr. Haydock, here is yesterday's 'Picayune.'" And he gave him the newspaper.

"For me!" cried Effie, amazed.

"For you!" cried Hester.

And Effie broke open her letter.

FROM MRS. LE CLERC TO MRS. E. ABGAR.

ARCADIE, Wednesday Evening.

MY DEAR MRS. ABGAR, — I have only to-day learned that you are to be in our neighborhood with your friends, and I write, although in haste, to beg you not to pass us on your way down the river. I know very well how much of pleasure you have before you. But surely, after your long journey, you will need some rest, and I cannot but hope that you and your friends will stay with us long enough to secure it.

Really, although our life is very simple, there will be a good deal here that will be new to you; and, at the least, we can assure you of a cordial Southern welcome.

Do not feel as if we were strangers. I must know many friends of yours among my Northern friends, and our friend Miss Ferguson, who is as eager as I am that you shall stay with us, feels sure that her niece was at Miss Sutphen's school.

Be sure that your visit will be to us a very real pleasure. My husband will be on the levee to welcome you as the " Boone " comes in.

Very truly yours,
ADELIE LE CLERC.

"That is hospitality," said Effie Abgar, after she had twice read through the letter, and made sure that it was indeed for her.

"How in the world did they know we were here?" said Hester. "I know, Effie. They must have been friends of that nice Mrs. Cheyne in Louisville. She said she had a sister on the coast; and I did not know what 'on the coast' meant."

Then Effie had to speak, though she knew she

crimsoned as she did so. "I do not think they are Mrs. Cheyne's friends. They are Mr. Brinkerhoff's friends; and this is the Arcadie he described. Is it not so?"

"Certainly it is," said he, frankly. "There is no mystery. You said you could not go without an invitation. I cannot but hope you will go, now you see how much pleasure you will give."

"It would be very churlish to refuse so kind a request," said Effie, quite carefully. "Do you not think so, Hester?"

And both the gentlemen stepped forward to ask the pilot a question.

"Effie," said Hester, in a whisper, "if you think it right, I should like to go of all things."

"Think it right?" said Mrs. Abgar. "It would be almost rude to refuse."

So they asked the gentlemen at what time they should pass the house. Not till after midnight! But if Mr. Le Clerc were waiting for them in the cold, all the more rude to pass by! The gentlemen went down and made the arrangement with the captain.

And Effie Abgar felt, that in her first trial of strength with this modest, thoughtful, determined Hiram Brinkerhoff, she had come off second best.

And she was not sorry.

CHAPTER X.

THE mystery of the invitation is easily explained. The moment Mr. Brinkerhoff had found that he had begun at the wrong end with Mrs. Abgar, and that her New England sense of the proprieties was entirely shocked by the idea of appearing anywhere uninvited, he had walked to the clerk's office and had written this telegram to Mrs. Le Clerc:

"Mrs. Abgar and party are on 'Boone.' Would you like to see them?"

He had given his negro attendant the despatch, had bidden him pull across the river "like fury," and deliver it at Chicot at the telegraph office. A silver half dollar, in those days an unusual sight, had stimulated the boy. Fortunately for Hiram, he had written from Cincinnati a full letter to Mrs. Le Clerc describing the picture gallery and the ladies they met there, and had gone into some little detail about them and their plans. Thus was it that she was well prepared to write her courteous invitation, when, within two hours after his despatch was written, she received it at Arcadie.

Of course the kind letter involved a change of plan. The ladies had to pack their trunks Friday night instead of Saturday morning. Fred Haydock hesitated whether he would or would not accept Hiram's invitation to stay at Arcadie as his friend. But at last the doubtful scale decided in favor of staying. He could not bear to bid Hiram good-by that night perhaps for fifteen years more. If they parted now, Heaven only knew when they should meet again. So the friendly captain was informed that all four would leave the boat at Arcadie.

The friendly captain was not sure that he should know which plantation was Arcadie, nor was the friendly pilot. As for Mr. Le Clerc's name, there were three or four gentlemen of that name within twenty miles of each other on the "Coast." So now Effie and Hester began to be afraid that they should be left at midnight at a strange plantation, where the lady did not even know Hiram Brinkerhoff when she saw him. The disgrace of such an accident overwhelmed Effie, whose imagination was brilliant enough to forecast every step of the mad adventure — the landing on a muddy levee; the poking along in the dark among howling curs and blind avenues, till they came to the back-door of the wrong house; the knocking, timidly, and then wildly, for entrance — the head poked out of a window — the cross question and the meek reply.

Why had she ever committed herself to an adventure so crazy! When she had once said "No!" why had she not held to it? What a goose to give way — only because a pretty note, in a nice hand-writing, on a neat sheet of note-paper, had been thrown on board the boat! Why had she not held to the regular etiquettes to which she was born!

But when some broken words of hers expressed such doubts, the wondering pilot turned his broadest face and kindliest smile on her. He bade her lose all fear. "We shall find 'em somehow," he said; but how he was to find them, in the darkness of midnight, with the river mist hanging over land and water, the pilot did not explain.

The news of so large a departure was, in its way, quite a shock to the little party in the ladies' cabin. But by ten all the other passengers had "told good by," as the Southern phrase has it; only Dr. Summerfield sat up a little longer.

In half an hour more, however, that worthy man parted from them, and then, hour after hour, the vigils continued of the four. The law of Natural Selection, which another generation called the law of "Elective Affinities," left Hester talking with Frederic and Effie with Hiram.

Twelve o'clock, and they talked.

One o'clock, and they talked.

Quarter to two, and a lad came aft to say, "The landing is in sight, ladies. You need not hurry. You have fifteen minutes before we are there."

"Then how in the world can the landing be in sight?" asked the impetuous Hester. And they all walked forward to see.

Far, far away as the boat rushed on was a speck of light. This the ladies were told was the signal on shore which Mr. Le Clerc had lighted to direct the pilot.

"How like Robinson Crusoe! I can see him in the picture, piling on the logs! Only no vessel came!"

There was a fascination for a minute or two in watching the speck. Then the girls went back for their traps; and, with shawl-straps, umbrellas and the rest, stood waiting. The boat rushed toward its goal faster than ever, it seemed. A few minutes more and they could see a white shed and dark figures moving to and fro. Nearer and nearer! There is no place along that steep shore where a boat cannot run up and land her passengers. Nearer and nearer! A gentleman with a lad behind him is visible, and three or four larger Negroes. Nearer and nearer! The great landing-plank of the larboard side swung round and hovered above the shore. "Ting! ting!" The pilot stopped the engines. Flash! from the depths appeared two great pine-knot torches, which, with the pine fire on shore, make the whole as light as day.

"All ready, madam!"

"Good-by! Good-by, captain!"

And the ladies ran on shore led by the gentlemen, fast followed by porters with trunks. An instant, and all are landed, the porters are back again, "ting! ting!" and the palace sweeps off, while the ladies and their friends are receiving the welcome of their new home.

"The boys will see to the trunks. It is so short a walk that I have no carriage here. Will Mrs. Abgar take my arm?—or which is Mrs. Abgar?"

So cordial, so thoughtful in every act were the father and son, that Effie's terrors were gone in a moment. In a merry party they walked through the gloom which settled on them as they left the pine fire. It did seem mysterious enough. Great trees concealed the stars from them, and how and why Mr. Le Clerc turned when he did, or bade her avoid this step or that, or found a gate to open, Effie did not know. But all wondering was short. In a couple of minutes they were on the steps of an immense veranda. The open door of a hall which was a hall, cheerfully lighted, invited their entrance. A lady stood in the doorway, and stepped cheerfully forward to say, —

"Welcome to Arcadie!"

"I am ashamed to appear at such an hour," said Effie, "and more ashamed now that you have been sitting up for us."

"My dear friend, it is nothing. Mrs. Le Clerc was sorry not to do so, but I would not let her. She is not quite well. And you must be so tired!"

The welcome, the simplicity and ease, and the beauty and completeness of every arrangement, made the ladies feel more at home than they could have believed possible. Glad to go to bed, of course, at two o'clock in the morning. But, as they pulled aside their mosquito nets, they could not but talk a little about the charm which seemed to have surrounded them from the moment the magic light had appeared in the distance. Palace after palace welcomes them on their travels. But in this palace one is so thoroughly at home!

And how deliciously sleep comes on when one does not hear the distant "thud, thud" of the engine, and when one's body from head to foot does not vibrate with the jar of the gigantic wheels!

The thoughtful Hiram had telegraphed to New Orleans for the letters which awaited the ladies there, and, as they sat at a late breakfast, these letters were brought in. Perhaps this seemed even more like magic to Effie and Hester than the roses and jasmines which were in fresh heaps around them. It did show how long was Mr. Brinkerhoff's arm, and how thoughtful his kindness. And Effie looked her gratitude to him when she understood at last that the letters did not rain down by miracle. Perhaps the one only thing in life that she had longed for, as she dressed herself, was that she might know that all at home were well.

While the Northern ladies sat reading their letters, the Southern ladies, one of whom was Northern too, fell upon Mr. Brinkerhoff in talk:

"And how is dear Mrs. Brinkerhoff?"

"Thank you. She was very well when I left her. I am disappointed that there is no letter from her."

"Is she as young and as lovely as ever?"

"I am sure I think so," said Hiram, blushing scarlet. "She is as busy as ever with her schools and her sewing, and her what not. I tell her she tries to run half the world."

"And why did you not bring her with you?" and so on.

Both Hester Sutphen and Effie Abgar afterwards acknowledged to each other, guiltily, that they drank in every word while they pretended to be reading letters of which just then they did not see one line!

But if they are ever to go to Texas the story must not loiter even in Arcadie. All the same they loitered there. The gentlemen had to tear themselves away after the second day. Uncle Sam's business and the business of Jeffrey, Petrie & Jeffrey admitted no more delay. Even Mr. Le Clerc's ingenuity could not pretend that the United States government needed Mr. Haydock at Arcadie or that Mr. Brinkerhoff would find large firms of retailers of drugs at the little village at the Post-office.

The ladies stayed longer. "Why do you

not spend the summer?" said Mrs. Le Clerc, very sweetly and frankly. "You say you ran away from that horrible snow and ice, only to be in a pleasant home. Shall you find any thing pleasanter than this in that murderous Texas?" And indeed Hester wondered at her own firmness that she said "No." For, as to Effie, she had not been firm. She had confessed that the plan of the party was none of hers. Arcadie seemed so lovely to her that she would have eaten lotos there as long as there was lotos to eat. And all the plan-making was thrown back upon poor Hester.

Before the gentlemen left, poor Fred Haydock was nearly beside himself, because he neither dared ask Hester's leave to stay for ever where she stayed, and, on the other hand, because he dared not go away without asking. So they came to the last afternoon, which was given to a party on the canal. The canal leads back from the river to a lake or bayou; how far back the explorers did not find. Nor did they care indeed. It was always afternoon to them, and whatever they saw was May!

In a great cart drawn by three mules abreast were many chairs, in which the ladies sat and rode, escorted by the gentlemen on horseback.

Then they arrived at a narrow canal, in which were a large and a small flat-boat. Haydock and Fred Le Clerc, who had made paddles for the occasion, went in advance in the smaller boat. The oldsters, with the little girl and her nurse, went in the large boat, towed by a negro man named Antoine, on shore.

The canal was only wide enough for the boat. On both sides were the most interesting and wonderful trees and shrubs and vines, perfectly green. Indeed it looked, as Mrs. Abgar said, like the pictures of Paradise, where they always mix up pines and palms and land and water. They saw no bears nor deer, though there are plenty there. But they did see, oh! so many beautiful birds! So they sailed for perhaps three miles more, with new wonders all the time. Then they came where a large cypress-tree had been felled across the canal! What was it to them? To sit still or to sail — it was all one! The pioneers rejoined them, and Effie made a nice, characteristic sketch, and then the learned said that it would not be afternoon any longer, and that they must turn their faces home.

But when they came back to the cart, lo! a chance for an adventure! Mr. Le Clerc's horse had broken his bridle and run away. Now the thoughtful Mrs. Le Clerc had arranged that Miss Sutphen should ride him home, because she had guessed that before Mr. Haydock left, he and Miss Hester would be well left together for an hour without listeners. Kind Mrs. Le Clerc! What perfect hospitality! And now? Why had this beast broken bridle? Fred Haydock, who generally believed in his star, and not without reason, could have groaned aloud — would have done so but that the manners of civilized society forbid. Did Hester care? *Quien sabe?* Wild horses would not have made her tell. With perfect willingness she seemed to acquiesce. Fred Le Clerc and Hiram both offered their horses, but not even Mrs. Le Clerc dared say that they could be trusted with an unskilful rider and the flutter of that rider's dress. Hester stepped up into the cart by the ready chair, begged Mrs. Le Clerc not to think of her nor be worried, assured Mr. Le Clerc that there was room for him on her seat, and so they took up their way, when, as the twilight began to gloam, a hurrah, a rapid movement, and the horse reappeared. He had run home, had been captured by a negro boy, and had been brought back in triumph. So he had six miles extra that day for his pains. The whole party stopped again. The side-saddle was exchanged for the Mexican saddle which Mr. Le Clerc had ridden. Fred Le Clerc and Hiram, after seeing that they were not needed, dashed forward to announce at home that there was no accident. Frederic Haydock and Hester Sutphen followed more decorously, and the slow cart, with its trijuge team, as Mr. Le Clerc called it, brought up the steady rear.

Hester tried her stirrup, tried her beast on different paces, tried a canter over a deserted field, tried a sober walk. She was indeed conscious that, if she and Mr. Haydock rode quietly side by side, a crisis was not far away.

And so it proved!

"Miss Hester, if that horse had not come back I should have died!"

"Then we are very glad the horse came back," said Hester. "But why were you responsible?"

"Oh, not that! I was not responsible. But all day long — oh, Miss Hester, do not laugh at me — all day long I have counted so on this half hour in which to tell you what you know so well."

And he was silent, and she knew she did know. But she said nothing.

"If it seems madness to you, let it seem so. If it seems foolish, let it seem so. But I cannot believe that I had never seen you before that day at Jersey City, and if you say I never must see you again — do not laugh now, Miss Hester — if you say that, I shall die. You have taught me a great deal in this fortnight. But you cannot teach me how to live without you."

Then Hester knew she must speak. The man had behaved manfully. He had his rights too. And Hester tried one sentence which would not come, and she tried another; and then she looked frankly up to him — only he could not see her in the darkness — and she said, in just her freshest, sweetest way,

"And why should I try to?"

Then how he thanked her and blessed her! Then how he promised her to be good to her and true to her and guard her as never woman was guarded! Then how he told her about his paradise at San Antoine; or, if she liked it better, he could and would resign and go back to New Hampshire with her. Then how they fell back upon the Palace life; and she asked him if he knew that they thought he was a girl and called him Honora MacPherson. And then the rattle of the mules behind was heard, and they had to whip up and keep out of the way with a pace too fast for talking. And then they came upon a good place to walk — ah me! all places were good to walk. Could they be all night in going home, it would be none too long. But the lights of the little homestead village would appear, and then the lights of Arcadie.

And when they came to the house the whole family must rush to the piazza to meet them, and one would hold the horse, and another would take Hester's whip, and Fred could only press her hand hard as she sprang to her feet. He could not clasp her round her waist, as he would have done had this been in the "Pirate's Companions" or the "Smugglers' Prize," and imprint a thousand kisses on her.

For, alas! the etiquette of modern society did not permit him.

But fortune favors lovers, favors the brave, favors the good, and favors the young! And Hester and Fred were lovers, were brave, were good, and were young! Fortune was so kind that, after every bag was packed, after tea was finished, after all had been said which must be said, except "Good-bye," the "George Christy" did not come. Now it was in the "George Christy" that the gentlemen were to go. And so they sat in the veranda or gallery, under the great colonnade, and waited for her, hour after hour. And lovely Mrs. Le Clerc, with all her skill in letting people alone, took care that neither Bob nor Fanchon should come near Mr. Haydock for stories, nor Miss Sutphen for paper dolls. Two hours — three — of solid comfort before the "Christy" came!

Did M. Le Clerc know or did he not know, did he guess, or did he not guess, — when he asked Fred to sing "Maudit Printemps," by way of illustrating something he was telling Mrs. Abgar?

"Maudit!" said she: "that is hard on poor Spring."

"Oh!" replied he, laughing, "that is only French fashion. It does not mean more than your Mr. Artemas Ward means by 'cussedness.' Fred translates it 'bothersome,' when he sings it in English."

So Fred sang, —

MAUDIT PRINTEMPS.

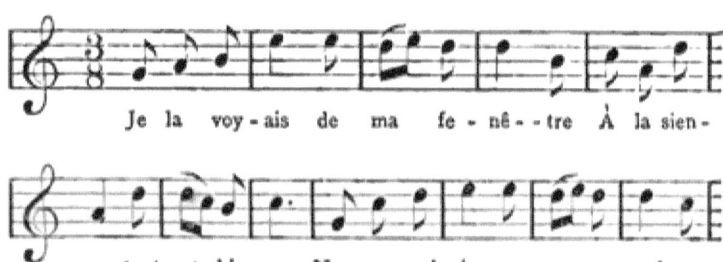

BOTHERSOME SPRING.

I saw her sitting by her door,
Half-hidden yonder mid the trees,
And though we never met before
Our kisses crossed with every breeze.
    Through naked boughs the winter through,
    From door to door the sight was plain,
    But now the leaves shut off the view:
    Oh Spring, why need you come again!
But now the leaves shut off the view,
Oh Spring, why need you come again!

But to Fred Haydock something else came as "bothersome" as spring. Even paradise cannot last for ever. At last a faint whistle up the river. The groups break up, and watch, and listen. A louder whistle and a louder. The plash of paddle-wheels.

"We had better walk to the landing!"

They all walked together; and the "Christy" came.

"Good-bye!"

"Good-bye!"

CHAPTER XI.

"BUT where is the Pullman all this time?" asks the indignant reader. "What do I care," he growls, "as to the loves or hates of Mr. Frederic Haydock and Miss Hester Sutphen? It was 'the adventures of a Pullman' which were promised to me. And now, all that I am told is the fortunes of a palace afloat and the hospitality of a palace not on wheels."

Reader, be still, and persevere.

For the week at Arcadie could not last for ever. And though they added six days more to it, those could not last for ever. If all had been stupid and dull, Hester would have thought it lasted for ever. But it was all light with kindness and love and new joy of spring, and new surprises of life unheard of by these Northern birds of passage. For Hester there was now a note from Fred, now a letter, now a telegram. Now a boat would run up to the levee, and a black man would run down to the landing-place, and find there a little parcel for "Miss Sutphen, at Mr. George Le Clerc's *Arcadie*," and Hester would carry it to her room and return with a blush, with the very volume of Hamerton which she had spoken of to Miss Ferguson, and which they had both forgotten, but which the faithful Frederic had not forgotten. Ah, me! how long are men's arms, and how strong, when they are enough in love.

Such weeks never last for ever!

So, when ended, the girls were kindly and tenderly put on the "St. Mary,"— a funny little stern-wheel boat, which was to go up the Red River. And their lonely life began again — but with such a chance to write long letters as perhaps the world gives nowhere else as it twirls round.

There could hardly be a greater contrast in life than the change from the airy comfort of the large bed-rooms in the luxury of Arcadie to these little six-by-six state-rooms of the "St Mary," the snuffy air and the cotton quilts. "Why they were ever called state-rooms," said Effie, "is something I never could find out, for there is less state about them and more Spartan simplicity than in any other place I go into." Still, when she wrote home, after a day's experience of the little boat, she said, "Happy is the country where the humblest emigrant going to the frontier has as good conveyance as we have. What you call the Law of Selection provides what everybody wants, even if it provide but little more. If there are few luxuries, there is still a good bed, a good table, and no end of kindness from these black men and black women around us."

For one generation, at least, no man need teach the black man or the black woman at the South, to be kind to the Northern traveller, — be that traveller whom he may!

The first day was Sunday. Yes, a quiet preacherless Sunday. The boat toiled on, as if indeed steam-engines were unknown to Moses, and not included in the comforts of the ten commandments. Yet the girls had their Bibles, — and Owen Feltham, and the dear old thumb-worn Fénelon, — and Vaughan's "Hours with the Mystics," — and Hester had a lovely talk with a nice Norwegian woman who could not speak a word of English, more than Hester could speak a word of Norwegian. But the fair-haired stranger produced her Norwegian Testament, and Hester had great joy in spelling out the blessings in the fifth chapter of Matthew, and then she showed her the same chapter in her book, in English.

And there was a piano on the boat, — where should one go as civilization advances unless he had a piano with him! — Why, you know it was behind the piano in the house in Kansas the other day that the panther sheltered himself till Mrs. Sloane could get her husband's breech-loader, and shoot him! and then, I suppose, while she was waiting for the men to come home from dinner, and drag out the ugly brute, she sat down and opened the piano and played an *adagio* by Schubert! So we live, as we face westward, — seventeen miles a year, as De Tocqueville says!

And Hester was just sitting at the piano after tea, and was wishing she had brought the Plymouth Collection with her, — and was trying one and another bit of old psalmody, — when the familiar signal for stopping the boat was heard, and it was announced that they had come to Bayou Sara.

Bayou Sara! How they had heard of Bayou Sara in old war days! Each of them had friends in the army who were at Bayou Sara. Hester's own brother was at Bayou Sara. But who Sara was or what a Bayou was, neither of them knew the more for this. No, Effie Abgar did not know, although Hiram Brinkerhoff had campaigned at and around Bayou Sara, and had told her so. The little bevy of ladies who had assembled around the piano to listen to Effie's playing, all adjourned to the guards, to see what might be the adventures of a stopping a little longer than usual. And then for a little they all walked at Bayou Sara.

In old prosperous times, which means before the war, the landing was the capital of a large and strong planting interest. It is now but a forsaken landing-place. As they walked, a wonderful sunset was going on; but they did not dare to linger long on shore. As the boat swung off again the stern wheel struck a floating log; and two of the arms, with the floats upon them, broke off, and floated down the river. This is to say that one sixteenth of the paddling power was gone, and the whole wheel weakened. While our friends were wondering whether this involved practically the end of their Red River voyage, the captain said to the pilot, "We shall put in new side-arms." Some one asked how long it would take to make the repairs. The Captain said, "Oh! about fifteen minutes."

In point of fact the boat's carpenter and his men went steadily to work. It was more than fifteen minutes, it was an hour, before the boat started again. Then the wheel was as good as new. Never was seen a more prompt and efficient piece of practical engineering. Allowing for the time in which they removed the wreck, they would have built a new wheel in four or five hours.

After such an adventure as this, the travellers looked with more respect on this quiet captain, whose place on the boat they would not so well have understood, but for some such exhibition of his power. Their friend, the pilot, was supreme in his department, and the ladies saw most of him. The mate, said to be the most amiable of men personally, appeared at every landing-place as the most vehement, not to say the most profane, director of the jolly crew of negroes who took the changing cargo on or off. The clerk evidently had his set of duties, which were not trifles. But if the girls had not seen the captain come to the front in some such trial as this of the demolished wheel, they would not have known what a captain was for.

A weirdly picturesque sight was the repair of the broken wheel. The sunset light failed fast. Instantly, almost without orders, one and another black man appeared with the long-handled iron baskets, filled with blazing "light-wood" and "pine-knots" which make the torches for all night work at the landings. The carpenters hung out over the water, working their wonders by the lurid flashes of these beacons. What amazed Effie and Hester was, that while everybody was in haste, nobody was in a hurry. Nobody scolded and nobody swore. Nobody half-did any thing. When the wheel was finished, it was finished. It was as good a wheel as if it had been made new at a ship-yard. All this gave them far more confidence in their bonny bark and her crew.

The ladies formed the habit of dressing long enough before breakfast to take a little walk on the deck above the saloon, by way of appetite. The morning haze, over the fresh green of the banks, gave a dreamy interest to the whole scene. They never tired of such mild adventure as a sharp turn in the river, coming back, perhaps after three or four miles, to the other side of some narrow neck, where was a cabin or a peculiar tree which they had seen long before, when they passed it on the other side. One morning, as they joined the pilot in his lookout, they mounted to the high throne reserved for visitors, who may look through the glass sides of the house, in every direction.

"And how far have we come in the night?" asked Effie. The pilot told her; and, with the science she had already acquired, she expressed her surprise that the run had been so short.

"The captain told me he should be opposite Nachitoches before this time."

"But the captain did not tell you, for he did not know, of that snag which we were to run into." This was the good-natured answer of the good-natured pilot. And in an instant he was sorry for it.

"Snag! snag!" screamed Hester and Effie. Neither had confessed to the other, or to any living being else, the terrors which the idea of "snags," whatever snags might be, had inspired.

Then the pilot expressed his surprise. He would not have told them, but he supposed everybody on the boat knew of it. It was between twelve and one that the boat had struck on a snag which was just near enough the water's edge to strike, not projecting far, the pilot thought, so it was not easily seen.

"Seen!" screamed Effie, "how should anything be seen between twelve o'clock and one in the night, with such a mist as this on the river."

"Anyway," said the good-natured pilot, "William did not see it. I was below," he added modestly. "Fortunately it did not strike the hull, only the after-guard. Look over the rail when you go down to breakfast, and you will see where it ripped the guard away. We dropped three hogsheads of sugar into the river. That will sweeten their coffee for them."

"Three of those great hogsheads into that muddy river! What a shame!" This was Hester's ejaculation.

But Effie, who had been peering over, said "How far aft was it?" And when the pilot told her, the ladies both understood that the snag had poked its head up, and the sugar had fallen through, just below the two state-rooms in which they had themselves been sleeping. Only they were such good sailors now that they had not been wakened — not much wakened. Yes. They had waked up. And they had heard voices. But each of them had thought it was a landing. And they confessed, each to each, that the comfort of feeling no throb of the engine, and of sleeping as one sleeps at home, had overcome all curiosity.

And so they had slept, one thin floor from death! They both went down to breakfast, solemnized, but not sad or unhappy.

The people who live on those narrow strips of

solid land between the upper Red River and the swamps behind it, above Nachitoches and below Shreveport, call it "the garden of the world." A great many other people call a great many other places the garden of the world. Let that be as it may, it is no wonder these people call this so. The strip is not wide. Sometimes it is a few hundred yards, sometimes it is a few miles, between the river and the swamps. But, narrow or wide, it is as fertile as so much land can be. Hardly an inch is wasted in fences. The long plantations were carefully cultivated to the very edge. And the girls unlearned their prejudices as to Southern laziness as they saw the work here. Effie asked a young gentleman whom they took from one plantation to another, how long the cotton planting season was. "Thirteen months in the year," said he laughing. "That is our joke about it. You see the fresh green yonder of this year's crop. These men have not been lazy, but you see the mule is trotting round in the gin-house yon; the last year's crop is not yet wholly made. This is not because they have been slack. To leave a part of that work till now may be in this case good farming."

Effie and Hester both remembered the "Raft" in their old geography days. It was over this

Raft that poor Will Harrod fared when he was escaping from the Apaches; — or were they Camanches? And what is left of the Raft, and what the pilot explained to them, did not disappoint them. The history of the Raft can be made out clearly enough by any traveller who passes up the stream. For there were places in the River not as wide as the steamboat was long, so that at those points she could not have turned round. For twenty miles, indeed, the river never seemed three times as wide as at these narrow points. If then, in some age, not long after the last deluge, maybe, in some ebbing freshet, which was bringing down masses of floating trees from above, two or three such trees happened to make what they call a "jam" at such a narrow place; if for two or three hundred years there happened to be no eager lumbermen, striving by hook and crook, by axe, saw, and crowbar to loosen this "jam," — why, of course, every new tree that floated down the river would pile in behind, but never a tree of them all would go down to the Gulf of Mexico. This is just what made the Raft. It piled up more and more, from year to year. It increased perceptibly on its upper end within the memory of the present century. At last it became in many places a bridge where you could walk across. The river would sometimes cut around it, would always flow under it.

So matters lasted till Uncle Sam, in his might, had leisure to stop and look at the Raft. It was then one hundred and thirty miles long. Uncle Sam sent Colonel Shreve with steamboats and toothpullers, of various kinds, and bade him abate the Raft. This was in 1836. Colonel Shreve did as he was bid, and now the river is open for hundreds not to say thousands of miles above the place where the Raft once closed it to all navigation.

It is hard to say what were the adventures of the ever-changing panorama, as the ladies watched the shores of the narrow river. Now some young gentleman in the pilot house threw a "Harper's Bazar" ashore to be picked up by the admiring group who watched the boat as it went by. Who was the "she" for whom the "Bazar" was whirled so deftly? Now it was a mountain of bags of cotton-seed, which would have staggered the might of Afrites, which the good-natured deck hands had to land under the persuasion of the eager mate. Now three little lambs strayed from an intelligent mother in that exquisite park where they were grazing, and stupidly ran down upon the beach, so to call it, below the little bluff. How stupid lambs are! The poor frightened mamma runs along on the crests, but cannot tell them to turn round, and escape the way they came. How stupid sheep are! Narrower grows the beach and narrower. Will they never, never return to their mother? At last one makes a bold venture, and scrambles up the bank! Safe! Then number two! Safe also! But here is number three, stupidest of all, will dear little number three be drowned?

Ah no! The intelligent pilot, equally interested with the ladies, gives one scream from his whistle; and, in an agony of terror, dear little number three rushes up the bank to the welcome of its mother.

Dear lamb, there are always friends watching us whom we do not know. And the terror most terrible, may be a friend in disguise!

"Effie! Effie! wake up, Effie! we are at Coshatta?"

This was Hester's cry to Mrs. Abgar as she took her constitutional and regular siesta after dinner.

"And what is Coshatta to me, or what am I to Coshatta," said poor sleepy Effie, dazed or dozing as you choose, when she emerged at the outward door of her state-room. Observe, untravelled reader, that each state-room has two doors. You step into the saloon, or out upon the guards, according as you go to dinner or to see a landing.

"Effie Abgar, I am ashamed of you. You did not know whether Campté was an Indian mound or a city, and now you do not know what Coshatta is. Yet Coshatta furnishes, let me tell you, every year one four-hundredth part of the cotton of the world. The chances are, therefore, that, as you press your head upon your pillow, one two-hundredth part of the cooling surface, is from these ports of shipment. I am not wholly certain indeed whether you ever heard of Shreveport, the place of our destination. From that port one-fortieth of the cotton of the world goes in search of its market."

So the ladies began to take some interest in cotton, and to learn how it was that people ever thought cotton was king. Here they took cotton seed on board to land it there, where was some new plantation. Here was a plantation wholly owned and run by new-made freemen. There was an old plantation on its mettle to adapt itself to the new order. Everywhere was diligent care, and, while the boat was at the landing at least, vigorous labor.

They went creeping up among the cotton plantations all day, stopping often. They expected to get to Shreveport that night, but the fog settled on them so heavily at sundown that the friendly captain had to tie the boat to a tree, and they must spend one more night on board.

Not so bad, as the friendly captain said, as his mother's experience. She was forty days coming from New Orleans, and only came to the Raft then!

So in one last social singing party ended their last day in "the garden of the world." How little they had thought that they should ever feel at home on the Red River! But there certainly was a homesick feeling about parting from it. Here was nice Mrs. Ritshey and her pretty daughter, here was poor Miss Harnett, who had such a sad limp, but was so patient about it, here was the droll little French bride who could not understand a word of English, though she were Hester's and Effie's fellow countrywoman, born under the American flag, and under that flag to live till she should die. With all of these ladies our travellers had come to be intimate. They had sung together at night; they had copied each other's patterns; they had borrowed each other's novels; they had taken each other's advice, and told each other confidential secrets. And now they were to part, and "never, never to see each other any more."

And here was the nice Norwegian girl who had come to regard Effie and Hester as her guardian angels, and who had now only two hundred miles more to travel before she met her lover, who had travelled a thousand miles to meet her.

They all met for one last good sing before going to bed, — French songs, Yankee songs, German songs, Texan songs, psalms, and hymns, and spiritual songs, and the Norwegian girl contributed her

NORWEGIAN SONG.

> My lover sailed away,
>   Far, far beyond the sea;
> But, on the parting day,
>   He gave a ring to me;
> And he said, "If God should make
>   My grave beneath the sea,
> This ring will snap and break,
>   For I'll ne'er come back to thee."
>
> He kissed me and was gone
>   Far, far beyond the sea;
> And I am left alone
>   For he's not come back to me.
> I have heard of storm and wrack,
>   But his ring is safe with me;
> So I know he will come back
>   To the ring he left, and me.

And with this pretty omen, if any one had understood the Norwegian, the party broke up for ever.

The next morning early they were at Shreveport.

CHAPTER XII.

OUR party was in no hurry. So Effie and Hester slept till morning, though the boat was at the landing long before. Mrs. Ritshey had gone, and the Harnetts had come, met Miss Harnett, and had taken her away, and only the Norwegian girl and the two friends were left, of all last night's party. There was no Mr. Haydock, alas! and no Mr. Brinkerhoff, as at friendly Louisville. But they were treated with all the honors, the luggage was all ticketed, and they evaded all coachmen, and walked with Lisa to the hotel where she must wait till the hour for her train.

Then the girls themselves had some hours, and these they lounged away as best they might. A chance to buy india-rubber and gamboge, and court-plaster, and note-paper, and French chalk, and hair-pins, and every thing else to make one comfortable! Walking out of town for purposes of sketching proved not so easy. It had rained heavily in the night, and the red mud of Shreveport was as tenacious potter's clay mixed in with Upton's glue, when the same has been well made by King. When they first crossed a street, Effie's overshoe was drawn off, as if some underground bull-dog had bitten it. It was only recovered by a resolute double-handed pull by Hester, and "that day they crossed no more"—streets. They retired to the station-house, made their sketches there, and with a paint-knife cut off the mud which still clung to the overshoe.

And then, early in the forenoon, the train. Not yet the Pullman, eager reader! At first only a comfortable airy car—but, oh, the luxury of seeing rolling hills and valleys again! Hardly hills. No, not high hills—but woods and slopes a little like home—and something not quite flat. So they came to Marshall, and here, after dinner, swept along the imperial "through train," ready to pick up such insignificant loiterers on branches. How ashamed the people who had not been running on express time were expected to feel!

But they were not ashamed. Effie gathered up the "Gray's Botany," the Official Guide and the Racine, her shawl-strap, her umbrella, her water-proof and her hand-bag, and with two hands carried them, and at the same moment held up her skirts. Hester picked up her Black's "Phaeton," Effie's sketch-book, her own portfolio, in which, when the train came, she was writing just a line to Mr. Haydock; she took also her cloak, her india-rubbers which she had not time to put on, and her carpet-bag, in her two hands. A cheerful black boy followed with their other "traps," and so they crossed to the platform of the imperial through train. Here stood a person who seemed not quite a stranger. "Here's your drawing-room car! Drawing-room car, madam!" And then he smiled a broader grin than before. Effie gave him her traps and mounted the steps of the Palace, not recognizing. Hester had a moment more to look on him. It was Aurelius, their own porter, who had left Jersey City with them — how long ago it seemed! And the Palace — it was their own dear Golconda!

"Home again, home again, from a foreign shore."

And they passed directly to "six and seven," and bade Aurelius put their "things" there, and sank into their old seats, after all their strange and eventful wanderings, with a delight which none can know but monarchs who have returned to the serene splendors of their own homes.

Do not ask me how the "Golconda" came

there. I do not know, nor did Aurelius know. Some hot box on the Iron Mountain Road above had disabled the "Siberia," and the "Golconda" had been substituted. And Aurelius, like the faithful lackeys of all palaces, had gone where his dynasty had gone, and was a Texan to-day as he had been a Jerseyman four days before.

And in more senses than one Hester and Effie felt at home. The country of Eastern Texas, where they now were, is not the rich and fertile region of which Texas boasts most. But these ladies had seen their fill, for the moment, of fertile lands. And what pleased them here, was that as one rode, this looked like the woodlands of Eastern Massachusetts, or of unmountainous Rhode Island. Of course the flora differs, but a pine is a pine, and though the skilful Hester knew and the keen-sighted Effie perceived that these pines were not their pines, still they were glad that they were pines at all. There were rolling hills, and railroad cuts enough to keep up the general resemblance.

It was no such country that the torrent of emigrants had come to see, and they were sweeping on further. The existence of the Palace car in such regions makes all other cars "second-class" and a wild enough look, unkempt and untidy have the body of passengers in them. They have slept in these seats, perhaps they have eaten in them, and have drank in them, and have made in them such toilets as they make. And they are of every country that emerged from Babel. Chinaman, black man, red man, Hungarian, Austrian, Prussian, Frenchman, Spaniard, Englishman, Scotchman, Welshman and Irishman, Jews and Proselytes, Cretes and Arabians, might all meet in one of these emigrant trains. The ladies would visit them sometimes to carry an orange or a banana to some of the tired children. And they were learning, all the time, how true it is that their own country is one out of many.

It will never do to try to follow along their diaries, with their vain and vague attempts to sleep off wheels at night, that as they rode they might see spring-time, the first real spring-time they had ever seen, in beautiful Texas, — where, if anywhere, spring is spring. The trouble of all such steps, in the Western system of travel, is this. There is but one fast train a day. That is, there is but one "lightning express." What is called a "fast train" on the schedule, may, very probably, be the slowest train of all. If then, you leave the lightning express at 11h. 55' to-day, it will be to take it again at 11h. 56' to-morrow, or any subsequent day for the next year that you may choose. If you take another train, at another hour, it is, most likely, only to be overtaken by the lightning train before twenty-four hours have gone. And you must sacrifice your Palace if you cease to ride on the lightning.

For all that, and for all that, the two travellers did alight at Hearne. Do you remember in the old geographies "Arctic Ocean, seen by Mr. Hearne?" He must have been another Hearne than this Hearne. This unknown Hearne has given his name to a place where the H. & T. C. crosses the I. and G. N.; and, if you do not know what that means, it is not my fault, but the crime of the teacher who taught you geography. And here, on a level prairie, is a station-house, which is what people there call a hotel, what in old Yankee times, men would have called a tavern, and there are the other accessories of a junction.

And here, on a lovely morning, the girls took their lives in their hands, and also took the botany books, and the sketch-books, and the colors, and walked into the Infinite. You cannot do this long when you start from a beach, because you find the water cold, and you must come back to the Finite. On a prairie you can keep on longer. Fences were left at once. Tracks of cows vanished soon. And then blazes of yellow flowers, flushes of pink flowers, blue streaks of flowers unnamed, all lapped in the eternal emerald green. Not without clumps of trees, oh, ignorant Yankee! and in such a clump the girls encamped, and took out the paints, and blotched in pink madder, and rose madder, and Naples yellow, and all the yellows, and tried all the greens and purples, and indeed all the colors of the prism, in the hope to carry something home of the glories of a prairie in spring. Such a morning! Think how they would never have known what they lost had they not spent that morning in Hearne!

Just a word here for the clean napkins, and bright spoons, and crisp radishes, and thoughtful table service of their dinner there! But we must not stop — no, not for dinners or for flowers. On and on, on and on, till we are waked our second morning as a chattering Englishman wakes his wife in 8 and 9, saying that "It's very like a park at home, my dear."

"I don't want to live here!" was her wretched groan in reply.

But perhaps she changed her mind afterwards.

For Effie and for Hester — though half Hester's heart was in St. Auguste — Austin had a thousand charms. No! nobody could call that hotel a palace, though Austin is the capital of an empire. But the friends who took care of them, the pretty homes, the lovely gardens, the charming drives, made them forget the hotel, which indeed, from morning to night, they hardly saw. What fate had bent them to go to San Antonio? Why not find some quiet lodging here, a little out of the streets of Austin, and nestle down for the spring-time, the sketching, the painting, for the rest which they had been madly pursuing so long? Just as at Arcadie, it seemed so stupid to go farther. At Austin it seemed as if they had all they asked for when they left home.

All Austin was crazy about the choice of a United States Senator. Not that anybody seemed to care much about United States politics. But here was an honorable post, for six years, to be given to some one who deserved well of his country. "Ah, Mrs. Abgar," said a gentleman to Effie, "ten years hence you will not have to trouble yourselves who shall be your president. We will choose him for you in Texas!"

In truth the population of the Empire of Texas doubles every five years. In 1870, it was eight hundred thousand; in 1875, they say it was one million six hundred thousand.

The hotel parlor brought together all the nationalities of the world again, as different people, of rather higher social grade than the girls had seen on the trains, were making their arrangements for new homes. What a *répertoire* of music that piano repeats as the year goes by!

Here were the English family, whom the waiters would call the Member of Parliament; here were some Italians, from Memphis, strange to say, not from Genoa; here were gentlemen and ladies from the ends of the earth. And the scrap which Effie wrote down, her last night in Austin, was not a camp-meeting song, nor a ballad of the Brazos, but a little air of Verdi's. All the same, he who sang was an American born, while he sang in the only language he had ever heard at home.

La donna è mo-bi-le qual piuma al ven-to,

mu-ta d'ac-cen-to e di-pen-sie-ro. Sempre un a-

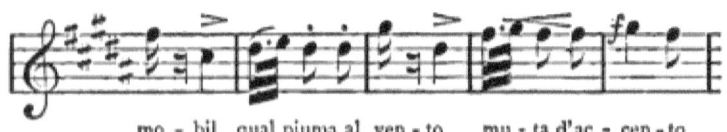

>   Woman is changeable!
>   Light as a feather,—
>   False as fair weather,
>   Who can believe her?
>   Always a beautiful face so beguiling,
>   Weeping or smiling,
>   Yet a deceiver!
>
>   Woman ah woman!
>   Light as a feather!
>   False as fair weather,
>   Who can believe?

Oh, it is misery!
Fondly confiding!
Tamely abiding
  Her fickle fancies,
Always felicity
Mocks the pursuer,
Whom as her wooer
Love ne'er entrances.

Woman ah woman!
Light as a feather!
False as fair weather,
Who can believe?

CHAPTER XIII.

PLEASE to observe that, in distance, from Shreveport to Austin these ladies had travelled about four hundred miles, say as much as the width of France from the Bay of Biscay to Switzerland. But they had not crossed half of the Empire of Texas, for Texas is an Empire; and, by the way, be it said, she knows she is.

Who were these ladies then that they should stay, even in the prettiest garden in Austin, or waste a month on its pleasantest verandah, and go home to confess that they had not gone half across Texas. They must see some Mexicans! They must know a ranchero by sight! They must walk and talk Spanish.

For San Antonio they had started, and to San Antonio they would go. They would show they were not women to be turned about by every word of friendship.

" 'The zeal that drove them from their native home
 Shall drive them gadding round the world to roam.' "

said the wretched Effie, parodying Dryden, as

she packed a pot of sensitive plants in a safe place among her spring bonnets and laces in the agony of the late Sunday night before they started across the prairies. That kind Judge Treadwell who had done every thing for them so carefully had engaged an ambulance and a driver who was to take them to San Antonio. "If the man were my own brother, Mrs. Abgar, I could not trust him more implicitly than I trust Dustin. I have sent Mrs. Treadwell and the children with him over the prairies a hundred times. I do so wish I could go with you!" So they were really to go in "an ambulance."

"Any thing, my dear Effie," said Hester, "so it be not a stage-coach."

For since Hester's wretched failure in taking care of herself on this great party, she had subsided ignominiously, and she was no longer the chief of the expedition. Effie made all the arrangements now. The pretence that either knew an inch of the geography had been long since abandoned.

At half-past seven an eager waiter at Hester's door announced that the "ambyourlance" had come. Hester flung the door open, bade him strap her trunk and take it down, gathered 1, 2, 3, 4, and took them herself, fairly ashamed of her own eagerness to see what manner of machine an ambulance might be.

She found simply a long canvas-topped wagon, lightly sprung — such as she had ridden in, on the White Mountains, twenty times, and had never heard called an ambulance before. There were but two seats in it, where there might have been three; but, as the party was so small, the middle seat had been taken away to make the more room for the luggage. Half amused and half provoked with herself, she turned to meet Effie and see if she would confess to any surprise.

"Is this an ambulance? I supposed there would be a bed in it, and that I should lie in it all day, and you sit by my side in the costume of Florence Nightingale to feed me with paregoric."

A little crest-fallen, they hurried through the last breakfast at Austin, and then, to the relief of the good-natured Dustin, the tall Pennsylvanian to whose escort they were entrusted, they mounted their chariot and were away.

A lovely morning! "Why, it is really May-day, Hester, of all the days in the year!" The air fresh and even bracing, the sun just clouded without the slightest risk of rain. Dust laid; who shall say how? since no rain had fallen for weeks.

Light hearts, light freight, a cheerful driver, and a good team, who could ask for a better way to spend May-day?

Effie's first chance for a sketch — and that only the barest suggestion of values and of groups — was as you leave the city at the ford of the Colorado. When the river chooses to rise, and nobody knows when that will be, it is twenty-three hundred feet wide. On this May-day it was perhaps sixty yards across. The horses were to be watered before crossing it, and at that moment a drove of beautiful cattle, a drove to fill Rosa Bonheur, nay Juno herself, with rapture, chose to file across the river at just middle distance from them, so prettily grouped, and the varied figures standing out so well against the water and the distant sky-line! Then the ambulance was to ford as soon as the "stage" had gone by. Neither of the girls had ever forded a river. At the bottom of each heart was sober certainty that they should be swept into the Gulf of Mexico. But each was ashamed to tell the other, and as in truth there was no danger nor shadow of danger, they could enjoy the wonderful picture all the way. A hard pull across the dry river-bed and then began the wonders of eighty miles' drive through a park of matchless beauty.

Yes, everybody says "An English park!" like the sturdy Englishman to his berth-dozed wife in the Pullman. High praise, to our English friends. Twenty years ago Robin said of these prairies, "Like a park;" good Mr. Flint keeps saying, "You would think you were in a park." That clever English woman, thirty years after, says "It is all like a park." And as the girls dipped into Mr. Olmsted's Texas from time to time they could not but ask whether inspirations from these Texan parks had not stolen since into the masterpieces of his success.

The road was perfect. It would not have been so after rain. But now the most sensitive critic could not ask any thing better. Sometimes it was fenced in, much more often not. Almost never was it exactly level, not once so steep but that the horses kept the even tenor of their trot.

"Oh, Effie! look here." "Hester, do look there." "See that distance; would you not be certain it was the sea?" "Was ever any thing grouped like those trees?" "Had you any idea that a prairie was so beautiful?" "Do you suppose this is a *bona fide* prairie? there are so many trees." And so on, and so on.

And then the flowers! May-day indeed. Hester had been in Switzerland at the end of June, years on years before, and often had she raptured to Effie about the day's ride, in which they collected a hundred varieties of flowers, most of them new to them. Here was the same experience in a new form. And these were not horrid coarse things, as people say prairie flowers are. Any one of the succession of the nosegays which Tom Dustin gathered for them, or which for themselves the girls gathered in one or another irrepressible escape from the carriage, would have been a beauty and a joy in any competition with any collection. Mistress botanist Hester, prime botanist extraordinary to the expedition, was beside herself for names, and the well-battered "Gray" lying in the bottom of the wagon proved of more use to press things in, which were to be sent home to Letitia to soak out in water and analyze, than for a guide in nomenclature. The "Gray" stood bold to its determination to pass no limit "south of Kentucky and Virginia."

"He won't pass it," said Effie, proudly, "but we have."

This list may well be compared with the lists of Swiss travel. Dividing by old Ransom's floral system, in which there were nine classes of flowers based on the several tints of the rainbow, there were, to use his language:

1. "Them as bears the white blossom." In this class was the original Eupatorium of Ransom, and two or three other varieties! Be it said to the unlearned that when a botanical writer wants to say he has seen a thing himself, he marks it with the mark of exclamation (!), and when he doubts the remark of another he appends an interrogation (?). The girls, as they made their list, when Dustin was watering or at other writing spots, delighted in the immense ejaculations which lighted it up.

It went on.

2. "Them as bears the violet blossom."

"Is magenta violet?" "No, child, magenta is red. Are you color blind?" "Then I shall put in purple lupine and false lupine here." "Put in what you choose. You already see the radical error of Ransom's system." But down went the two lupines with two marks of wonder!! And purple verbenas, of which there were acres on acres of color, had to come in here.

3. "Them as bears the indigo blossom."

Hester was blank here. She had only two or three vile hyssops which she could have gathered in any barnyard. But when they came to

4. "Them as bears the blue blossom," she put down lupines and blue verbenas. "What is that

about that Horticultural Society which offered a prize for blue verbenas? Was it all humbug; or why did not somebody come here and win the sordid dross? Here I must put in many surprise marks to show my scorn of the older observer."

But these things were only preliminary. "Blue flowers?" said Hester, "I always distrusted blue flowers. My verbenas at home always had a passion for running into the class of purples, though I never got the prize." It was not till she came to her reds that she ran rampant.

This magenta blossom which she wanted to put in first, which the maidens of the region call "wild Hollyhock," the painted cup — only red reminiscence of New England — the Star of Texas, an exquisitely cut flower of very delicate pink, these were alone enough to give dignity to class No. 5 of the Ransomic system. So different from lands where the ruling color is yellow on grass!

But, when the girls had come to "Class No. 5," their classification ended in their first reasonable access of terror.

Judge Treadwell had not told them that, ten days before, the mail-coach had been attacked by highwaymen, and all their watches and money taken from the passengers.

But this was really the reason why he had entrusted them to Dustin and an ambulance. The "private team" is safer because nobody knows it is coming.

Effie had seen on a hand-bill in the post-office offering a "REWARD" that the mail had been robbed. But she had not mentioned it to Hester.

Hester had seen the same "Reward" offered in a Galveston newspaper. But she had not shown it to Effie, and had torn the paper to bits lest she should see it.

Dustin was no more anxious about the matter than he was at the danger of a thunderbolt because he had heard of thunderbolts. But he had too much sense to speak of it to the ladies.

All the same, however, when, as he gathered up his reins after watering the horses, looking back on the Eastern horizon, he saw two men, perhaps two miles away, pressing their horses towards him on a hard gallop, Dustin stepped back into the ambulance rather too hastily. And he gave the horses rather an untimely and ungracious cut. For Dustin meant to push them beyond the strip of wood-land which they were entering before these horsemen overhauled him.

It was in this very strip of wood-land that the mail had been overhauled.

The sun was now setting, as far as ever in advance of them, though they had travelled towards him so long.

The accent of Dustin's cry to his team was unfortunate.

Hester, more nervous than usual, perhaps, caught the alarm. She had noticed his look back and the sudden change of his manner. She thrust her body out of the carriage, looked back, and saw the horsemen against the eastern sky.

"It is the robbers! It is the robbers!" she sobbed, as she fell back.

And Dustin did not say her no. But he "cut" the horses again with that same merciless lash which the ladies had never seen before.

Effie Abgar thrust her body out on her side. She saw the two horsemen also.

She said no word. But she detached her watch and chain, she wrapped them in her handkerchief with her purse, and she crowded the whole into the bottom of the bag of corn which Dustin had for his horses. She bade Hester do the same with hers.

A stern chase is a long chase. And the two bays understood what was expected. The road was rougher in that thicket than in the open prairie. But the ambulance held together, even though it sprang wildly from side to side, and sometimes toppled fearfully as if it would go over.

Dustin only spoke to his "cattle." And the girls said no word to each other or to him.

But they knew what he thought the exigency when they saw the horses break into that wild run from the quick trot before, unchecked by him.

Up a little slope — round a curve in the timber. Then Dustin spoke, —

"When we have rounded yon oak, mum, we shall be in sight of Tremlett's, and all's well."

But yon oak was fearfully far away! They had not reached it, no, nor half reached it, when they could hear horses' hoofs behind them.

Then they could hear voices, "Hold up! Hold up! Tom Dustin, hold up!"

But Tom Dustin this time really swore at his horses, though he had never been known to be profane before, and cut more unmercifully than ever.

"Rat, tat, tat: rat, tat, tat" — how fearfully near the hoofs came!

And at last, though the road was narrow, a white horse dashed by them.

"Will you hold up, I say?"

CHAPTER XIV.

IN all narratives of adventure, there is, at the crisis, one satisfaction for the reader; viz., that he can judge by the mere number of pages between him and the end of the book, whether there be any thing more to tell. Whether a given earthquake engulfed all the persons of whom the book has treated, or only one half of them, or possibly only one quarter, may be roughly determined by the rule of three. And thus, most skilful readers are aware, that in the real tug and throe of a book, when the "Alert" is pinched hardest in the floe; or when nineteen lions, with mouths open, are ranged in a circle around Captain Cumming and his two discouraged naked Mnoongsa guides, — most readers, I say, are aware, that to themselves, "about one quarter of this book is yet unread, therefore about one quarter of the people in it still live." To persons who begin at the last chapter, and read backward, this calculation is unnecessary. But their system is so destructive, so injurious to all effects, whether of poetical justice as wrought out in nature and in fact, or of the deftly devised plot even of the most skilful novelist, that it is justly condemned in all courts of literary justice, where authors are the arbiters. The true formula, as has been said, for discovering the exact annihilating power of any earthquake, epidemic, hari-kari, rise of a tidal wave, undrained village street, collision of trains, or, as in our little book, an attack of banditti, will be found in the following equation:

$$x = \frac{nc - pc}{p}$$

Where x represents the number of survivors after the crisis, c the whole number of characters, p the number of pages read, and n the number of pages in all.

It is only when Messrs. Longman or Messrs. Roberts pad the end of the book with thick advertising sheets, that the average reader is misled by this formula. And this custom is so annoying, that in Sybaris, and in the Young Companions' Country, the custom of Utopia is still maintained, where, by statute, publishers were compelled to put the advertising sheets at the beginning of the volume.

In the case of the little adventure with which

our last chapter closed, the purposes of melodrama would have been better accomplished had the brigands succeeded in rifling the purses of the ladies and taking their watches. In very fact, only ten days before, two men on this same road, took nine watches from nine stage-travellers, two of whom were officers in the United States army; and, about ten days after, a similar event took place on the Southern road to San Antonio. If, at that point, Fred Haydock and Mr. Hiram Brinkerhoff had started out from a thicket, had killed two banditti with revolvers, and slain two by the edge of the sword, escaping themselves miraculously with only a slight flesh-wound in Fred Haydock's left arm, which Hester herself were permitted to bandage, this little story would have had just the element of romance which, alas, it has not; and these remaining pages would have had just enough of blood, of arnica, and of the Extract of Hamamelis to give them interest in the eyes of the general reader.

But, really, this was not what happened. So soon as Dustin saw the white horse pass him, he knew the game was up. He sulkily drew up his own beasts, and even swore at them because they did not stop as sharply as he wished them to do.

The other rider, on a bay horse speckled with the frothing of his own running, passed on the other side.

The two girls sat back in the ambulance with no feeling of terror now. Effie was conscious of the simple feeling of amusement, and Hester's was crude curiosity. "What would happen next?"

What happened was, that the bay horse was checked most easily, and his rider turned him.

It was Hiram Brinkerhoff who said, "I hope we did not frighten you." And then as he saw that the party had been frightened, he was abject and eager in his mortified apologies. But really the young men were not so much to blame. They had arrived in Austin only that morning. All their time there was spent in tracing the ladies, and they had been on one or two false trails. They had known nothing of mail robbers, and were both of them, sooth to say, so ignorant of Texas and its customs that they thought of such things as little as they would have done in East Orange or in North New Milan. As they dashed after the ambulance they were only afraid that some drunken driver had these two ladies in his care.

Poor Tom Dustin!

No, Lily! No, Emma! The measurement of the Town and Country series is pitiless, is remorseless. There must be no space wasted in these pages on what Fred Haydock did or did not say to the two ladies as he walked by the side of the carriage, while his horse followed meekly, and the cortège went down to Tremlett's. For of course with Hiram Brinkerhoff was Fred Haydock. Of course the one had seen his correspondents in New Orleans, in Baton Rouge, in Nachitoches, and had then hurried to Austin to meet his appointment with Fred. Of course the other had wound up all the government business in St. Auguste, and had hurried by Galveston to Austin to meet his appointment with Hiram. Hester Sutphen had unfortunately missed the telegram which begged her to wait till they came. So was it that while the girls going out from Austin were fording the Colorado, the two gentlemen were entering Austin in seats six and seven of the "Golconda."

Then, as has been said, they were on a false trail at first. None the less did they mount themselves well at Austin and went in pursuit, with what fatal success the reader has seen.

The ladies were forgiving, more forgiving perhaps than the gentlemen deserved. With much laughter the watches were disinterred from the bags of corn. On a sober walk all the steeds came up to Tremlett's. The people at Tremlett's were amazed to see Tom Dustin's team come in, in such a lather. But their curiosity was not appeased at first, and the young ladies were at once received, in the simple kindness of the hospitality of a wayside inn in Texas, to the cold water and other refreshment which should restore them from the terrors of the last hurried mile.

In the "gallery" hung a pail of water, because in a country where ice is unknown in May, the best chances for keeping water cool come, by maintaining for it a steady evaporation on every side. The gentlemen dipped from the pail, and made their ablutions there. Hiram even had a chance to open his ready sketch-book, and by one or two tints to give some of the effects of the sunset, when they were all summoned together to supper.

They found that they were not the only travellers. From one and another point different people assembled, and it proved that an extra stage had "put up" for the night, and that some wayfarers in pursuit of lost horses were here. The meal was served in a rough ell behind the house; and the several guests — some in their shirt sleeves, some in more full costume — gathered silently at the long table.

No one spoke. And, in a moment, the reason was apparent, as Tremlett, the innkeeper, at the head of the board bowed, and in simple language asked a blessing.

"Talk about godless Texas," said Hiram, afterwards, as he and Fred went to look after their horses' cheer. "It is the only region where I have ever travelled, where an inn-keeper asks a blessing, before his guests fall to."

A beautiful moon had come up while they were at supper. The air was clear as in a winter night in New England. The ladies sat a little while on the gallery, but then owned they were tired, and bade good-night, led away under Mrs. Tremlett's watchful care to see what manner of contrivances Mrs. Tremlett's beds might be. As the good lady lighted her "dip," she turned kindly to Hester, and said, inquiringly:

"You're from the East, my dear?"

Hester said she was.

"From Chicago?" continued Mrs. Tremlett.

"Oh! farther than Chicago," said Hester, laughing.

"From New York?"

"Oh! farther than New York. I am from Boston!"

"From Boston, be you," said the good lady, indeed surprised. "Then you speak French!" And so the mystery of Hester's and Effie's bad English and foreign accent were accounted for. This was not the only time in Texas when they found that their beloved "hub of the universe" was rated as in a foreign land.

Meanwhile, on the "gallery" gathered the different men-folk, travellers, or of the household, and as the number became too many for the chairs, one and another threw himself on the ground in front, basking, so to speak, in the full light of the good-natured moon.

"In my country," said Hiram, "I should hardly dare to sit out in the evening air, as we are sitting now, though it were the middle of August. And this is only the first day of May."

One of the young Texans replied that there had not been five nights since New-year when he would not willingly have slept on the ground there, wrapped in a blanket, so little risk was there from the dews.

"No dews, and no rain," said Hiram, "then what is it which keeps the prairies green?"

But this was what no one could well tell.

They said it was three months since there had been any rain-fall of consequence. Indeed, they said their springs were low and their crops suffering. Yet, as the travellers had seen, the prairies were as green as a mowing lot in Massachusetts would be a month later in the year.

All that anybody could say was, that the roots of the prairie grass were very long. This mesquit grass, for instance, which is such a blessing to man and beast, throws down its root three feet below the surface.

And then, in the midst of this geoponic lore, a long wagon drove by, with extemporized seats for eight or ten people, and they sang as they rode.

No-bod-y knows the trouble I've had, No-bod-y knows but

Je-sus. No-bod-y knows the trou-ble I've had,

Glo-ry, hal-le-lu! I felt the bur-den of

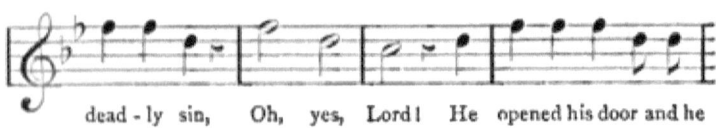
dead-ly sin, Oh, yes, Lord! He opened his door and he

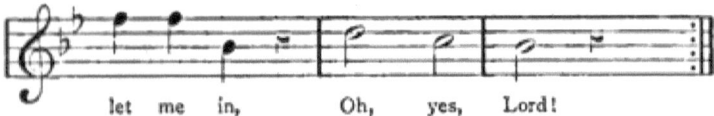
let me in, Oh, yes, Lord!

"They are going home from the camp-meeting at the corners," said Tremlett in explanation. One and another of the singers waved a hand as they went by. But the carriage did not stop. As it receded upon the prairie, successive verses of the song could be heard, less and less distinct, as the distance increased.

Nobody knows the trouble I've had,
Nobody knows but Jesus.
Nobody knows the trouble I've had,
Glory, hallelu!
I fell on the ground and I kissed his feet, Oh, yes, Lord!
And he lifted me up with his smile so sweet, Oh, yes, Lord!

Nobody knows the trouble I've had,
Nobody knows but Jesus.
Nobody knows the trouble I've had,
Glory, hallelu!
I took his hand and I held it fast, Oh, yes, Lord!
And I will hold it to the last, Oh, yes, Lord!

Nobody knows the trouble I've had,
Nobody knows but Jesus.
Nobody knows the trouble I've had,
Glory, hallelu!

I took his crown when his temples bled, Oh, yes, Lord!
For I heard the gracious words he said, Oh, yes, Lord!

Nobody knows the trouble I've had,
Nobody knows but Jesus.
Nobody knows the trouble I've had,
Glory, hallelu!
Oh, take my burden, and bear my yoke, Oh, yes, Lord!
These were the gracious words he spoke, Oh, yes, Lord!

And, after this, it was impossible to follow the verses.

The young gentlemen took the song as a consecration of to-night, and broke up the little bivouac to try the comforts, hardly so attractive, of Mrs. Tremlett's bedrooms.

CHAPTER XV.

WHEN morning came, it proved that a "Norther" had struck them in the night. But it was a very gentle "Norther" compared with what they had all read about in Mr. Olmsted's book, and in the adventures of Phil Nolan's friends, which, just at this moment was working along in Scribner's Magazine. All the hurt it had done anybody was, that everybody had wakened at four o'clock, and had pulled up his bedquilt. Blankets appeared to be unknown at the Tremlett's. But, in a cotton-growing country, quilts are quite as thick as any traveller will require.

When breakfast was ended, and the ambulance came round, it proved that Fred Haydock had bought a side-saddle from Tremlett; that Fred's own saddle was fastened behind the ambulance. So Hester very prettily yielded to Fred's eager request that for the first hour she would ride on horseback with him.

Was not it kind in Hiram Brinkerhoff to let her take his horse, while he jolted in the ambulance?

And Fred and Hester were able to go back to that first ride, so long ago, in the darkness of Arcadie!

Then, after an hour, they took the ambulance and Effie and Hiram rode in their turn. Just as they mounted, Dustin pointed to the southwestern horizon.

"A drove of cattle, Mrs. Abgar."

And over the slope, three or four miles away, Effie made out a long line of ants creeping in line of battle.

But in half an hour the travellers had neared the ants and the ants the travellers. The ants were an army, half a mile from flank to flank, of beautiful cattle. Oh, how Juno, or Minerva, or Aphrodite would have quarrelled for those white ones! Black, white, red, brown, gray, mauve, ashes of roses, salmon color, pink, mottled and pied — no two oxen alike — but all with a look not so strange, both of gentleness and vigor. They plodded amiably along; they cropped the grass as if they had been pet lambs, or, if they had loitered too long, they galloped when they were touched up by impatient drivers.

The drivers — wild bandit-looking men, with Mexican hats, and queer buckskin leggings — rode from end to end of the troop, almost at right angles with its line of march to be sure that no ox strayed behind. And so, in solemn procession, the twenty hecatombs of oxen were to march a thousand miles, from day to day, till they should ascend, not a sacrificial altar, but the trains of cars which should bear them to distant Brighton.

"You might tie a letter for your husband on the horn of that lovely white one, and he might find it at his butcher's, if he were romantic enough to ask for Texan beef."

So said Hiram Brinkerhoff, laughing. But even in the motion of the horses he could see that Mrs. Abgar started. What had he said?

She asked him, — coldly was it? — or with what tone? —

"I do not understand you."

"I say," said Hiram, red in the face, "that you could make the cattle your mail-carriers to your husband — to Mr. Abgar."

"Why, Mr. Brinkerhoff, I beg your pardon; it is all over now, but you surprised me. My husband has been in heaven many years. I never had a husband but for one happy month. People say it was too happy, but I do not think so." And she smiled with that beautiful sad smile.

Hiram Brinkerhoff was still crimsoned. "Dear Mrs. Abgar, pardon me. You know! I am sure you know I would not have pained you. But!— Well!— You do not see!— But you have spoken so much of Mr. Abgar, of Phil, you call him — I supposed — Mr. Haydock supposed —"

"Dear old Phil! yes," said Mrs. Abgar, her face not losing its sweetness. "Where should I have been but for him? He is my husband's older brother. But dear old Phil has a very charming wife of his own, and such lovely children! I thought I showed you their pictures."

Yes, she had showed their pictures, and had said they were her nephews and nieces, but she had not said that they were Phil's children.

It was queer: they could not justify it to themselves, nor in any way explain it. But there is no doubt that after this contretemps and explanation neither of the two cared to go on with the other, just then, in just the easy and confidential way in which they had ridden before. As soon as Mrs. Abgar's hour was ended she said she was a little tired, and she resumed her seat in the ambulance. Fred's horse was fastened behind, and Fred took the vacant seat by Dustin.

But Hiram Brinkerhoff did not propose to drive in Dustin's place, as he might have done, and they kept on, a broken party, till they came to Braunfels.

Dustin at one moment pointed forward with his whip to a great yellow square patch of — who should say how many acres? on a distant swell.

"Have they such wheat as that in your country, Mrs. Abgar?"

Effie liked to hear him talk about the wonders of Texas.

"No, indeed," said she. "We have no wheat in my country. But, Mr. Dustin, not even in Texas, I think, is wheat as yellow as that on the second day of May."

"Sure enough, mum, sure enough! It must be flowers, mum!"

And so it proved, when, after an hour's riding, they passed through this yellow patch, and found themselves surrounded by forty acres of coreopsis in full bloom!

But Dustin had his revenge upon Effie, as she was frank enough to confess to him. She had made a sketch, involving one of these sweeps of tremendous distance, and she had written in on it for use, if she could ever put it in color, across a little bit of her middle distance, "little pond quite as blue as sky." When they rode on and passed through the "pond" it proved to be a giant's patch of blue verbenas!

The exquisite, clear spring of the San Marcos River is a natural curiosity which all travellers must stop to wonder at. San Marcos itself was a wonder to them, because it was their first town after they had left Austin. Then Braunfels with its quaint German look, mixed in with southern traits, and unmistakable Americanisms, would have been an interesting place to stay in. But, no! they held on to their journey's end this time; and at last, when they were well tired, they came to the point where Will Harrod bade good-by to Inez Perry, and so through fresh mesquit trees dashed on till they saw all the crosses and spires of San Antonio. Does any one, by good luck, know who Will Harrod and Inez Perry were?

And in San Antonio they found all that they had come for. First of all, in the Menger House, so neat and comfortable a home. Then, when they had washed and rested, such a funny walk, where no one knew an inch of the way. Wherever they went they came to the river, — and a river "as is a river," — so active, so deep, so green, so satisfactory every way. "What funny little bathing houses! can people bathe in May?"

It seemed as if every garden ran to the river and as if everybody had a bathing house in his garden of his own.

None of them had ever been in Spain. But they supposed, and were perhaps right, that San Antonio looked like a little city in Spain, with these narrow streets sometimes made to give shade in summer, and with these white walls almost windowless, which make the sides of the streets.

Yet sometimes they came to a distinctive Swiss cottage, and sometimes it was the legitimate Southern house with its broad gallery. Still Spain preponderated. And the Spanish talk in the streets preponderated over the German and the English. And when the four stood in either of the squares, the Military Plaza, or the Cathedral Plaza, or the Alamo Plaza, it was impossible to believe they were in their own land.

A lovely sunset and a short evening before sweet sleep avenged and rubbed away the fatigue of eighty miles' drive across the prairies.

CHAPTER XVI.

THE ladies slept in the same room. In the confidences of the toilet, night and morning, Hester told Effie, yes, of fifty things which she and Fred had agreed upon in the long talks of the day and evening before. But Effie — she did not know why, though she made up her mind to it two or three times — did not tell Hester of the mistake of Mr. Brinkerhoff and of her discovery of it, and of the foolish way in which for the moment it had disturbed her. Mrs. Abgar did not need to take the trouble, for, the night before, Fred Haydock had told Hester Sutphen the whole of it. And Hester could not conceive how or why the two men should have been mistaken.

There had been some hitch about the expected letters the night before. But at breakfast the hitch was loosened, and the great stack of letters came in. To the gentlemen, not so many. To the ladies, galore. And over cooling muttonchops, and coffee which was cold before they were done they read, now silent and now aloud, with ejaculations of surprise.

After the ladies had finished theirs, Effie turned to Mr. Brinkerhoff, resolved to show that the stiffness of a minute of yesterday should not last.

"And what are your letters?" she said. "You have better luck than Fred has," — for by this time Fred had insisted that they should not call him Mr. Haydock.

"Oh! mine are all business, I am sorry to say, except this from my mother. She has sent me her picture, which she has just had taken at Meserve's. It is not nearly good enough," he added, fondly, as he gave it to Mrs. Abgar to look upon.

"It is perfectly lovely," said she, frankly, and with an artist's pleasure. "So friendly, and so young."

"But why does not Amy write to you?" said Hester Sutphen, beginning to take advantage of the newly born intimacies. "Is not there a word from Amy?"

Hiram Brinkerhoff looked puzzled, was puzzled.

"Why, this is 'Amy,'" said he, at last. "It seems foolish to you, but I do not know, when I did not call my mother 'Amy.' My father liked it. She liked it. And I am sure I liked it. It was a trick of a baby, and I never grew out of it when I was a man."

The girls would have given gold if they could have kept their faces unchanged. But they knew that blood flushed them. With the resolution of martyrs at the stake they looked neither to the right nor to the left. Effie Abgar said nothing — had nothing to say. But the recollection of speculations and discussions about what manner of woman Amy was would come back, even in that moment. Hester, because she was the interlocutor, forced herself to say, —

"Why, we took it for granted you were married; and, for one, I wondered why you never said a word about your wife!"

With this bold speech the conversation dropped for a moment. Fred Haydock would have given his hot omelette if he could have thought of any thing to say, but he could not. The pause was but for an instant, when Tom Dustin came in to ask if they would ride.

Yes, they would ride. And he need not drive them. Mr. Haydock would drive. And each of the four said to himself or herself that the botch about Amy was over, and that it made no sort of difference. And they ran up those queer stairways to their rooms round that Moorish courtyard, all saying to themselves, "It was all nonsense, and will make no difference." And when the girls came into their own room Hester kissed Effie and said, —

"Did you think I was such a perfect fool? For I did not till this morning."

"We were all fools for a tenth part of a second," said Effie. "But it will make no difference now."

Still, in her heart she felt it would make a difference. She understood in her heart of hearts, that she and this loyal, frank, thoughtful, experienced gentleman had been living together for many days, and she, for one, thinking much of him in other days, when they were not together, with an ease and a simplicity which would have been just possible, perhaps, had each been quite well informed as to the other, but to which, after these two blunders, it would be very hard to return.

Hiram Brinkerhoff had had nearly twenty-four hours to consider another question. And Hiram Brinkerhoff was well aware, by this time, that with this lovely, conscientious, unselfish woman, so kind and affectionate, so quick of observation, but so unconscious of her own quickness and tenderness, he did not want to be on the same calm, reserved or unreserved relation in which they had lived, while he had supposed her to be a married woman, resting herself from the cares of housekeeping, while she played the matron for her friend. But Hiram Brinkerhoff knew that he must somehow show himself worthy such a woman if he would win her. . And this, he knew, would take time.

Of the four he was perhaps the very cheeriest of all, as they entered the ambulance. But it was a lovely day. They were to see if they had found what they had come so far to find; and they were all cheery.

"I believe," he said, so soon as all were seated, "that we are to go and look for school-rooms for Miss Sutphen's school. I have in my pocket a list of unoccupied old court-rooms and vestries of churches. Indeed, if she will pay enough, she may have an old corn bin in the corner of the Alamo, which the government has been storing some musket-barrels in."

All this was his invention. There was no such bin, nor such musket-barrels. But this must be said, because some readers are dull.

"I thank you," said Hester, laughing. "But I

will not trouble you to look for rooms with me. I know all my friends may not stay till autumn. Let us go out to one of the Missions. I can confess there, and receive absolution, which I need. Meanwhile there seem to be enough children here."

The multitude of children in the streets of a city in which there is no system of general schooling, always amazes a New Englander.

So they asked their way here, and asked it there — and without losing it more than twenty times, they came to one of the "Missions." It was not the one they started for, but what difference did that make?

A great ruined church — a ruin as satisfactory as if it had been in Morocco or Spain. Big dogs had to be quelled — and from the door of a hovel came out a pretty, shy-looking Mexican girl with an immense bunch of keys. Yes, there is a consecrated altar still, and at fit times there is worship still. But who worships, it would be hard to say! For all this is miles away from the city. But this was once the active centre of one of those colonies of reduced Indians, *Indios reducidos*, which the Franciscans managed somehow to convert to habits of peace. Of Christianity in its other forms, it is said that they knew the sign of the cross when they saw it. And I am afraid they knew no more! Where are they now? *Quien sabe?*

It is a strangely fascinating place. A curious bit of careful carving here, two or three rough-hewn rails from a fence there; a pile of fallen stones, a crucifix and an altar. The inquiring shy Mexican girl — the inquiring eager New England woman! Are the two of the same race, and were they born into the same world?

There are, I believe, five mission buildings in all. You might see two or three in a day; but our travellers were in no hurry. There are wonders in the city as well — the archives to be hunted through, under Mr. Smith's kind help, for rumors about Aaron Burr — for the fate of poor Philip Nolan the elder — and in the hope of a trace of Inez Perry and her aunt Eunice. No end of thoughtful and kind hospitalities from the gentlemen of the army, from their wives and daughters, whose welcome to their homes made these stray travellers feel as if this were not a bit of Spain, not a scrap from Mexico — but that all that had been a dream, and they were all at home.

One of their friends took them to the head-quarters, and here they were most cordially welcomed. Here they saw the very table on which General Lee signed the great paper of capitulation at Appomattox Court House. "Had you ever thought they had marble-topped tables in such places?" And here were gentlemen who had been engaged in those long forced marches. Ay! and ladies who had been watching and waiting at home for those gentlemen. It was hearing history, indeed, to listen to the anecdotes of those days.

A thousand pretty hospitalities, a thousand funny adventures, when they did not know whether they were to speak German or Spanish, or the language of Pimos or Panis; loiterings in gardens, and scampers on prairies, — took up the time, and would have taken up a great deal more.

Only too fast, in the climate of paradise, slipped by the fortnight which was the furlough which the young men had granted themselves.

In the morning, after an early walk, the ladies would paint or draw, or press their flowers, or dissect them, or sew or embroider, and the gentlemen would read or draw, or talk at their sides.

In the afternoon, after a siesta, all four would ride. It never rained.

Dear reader, if you have a friend, who is a little hectic, — who begins to cough; and if the doctor begins to talk of a milder climate than that of Boston or Portland or Bangor, — think twice before you send him or her whom you love across the waters. While you are thinking, determine whether it be not better for an invalid to stay in his own country. Let him go to San Antonio, said to be the most healthy city in the world. Since these ladies went, a railroad has been finished. So that the invalid need not leave the "palace" till he arrive at his journey's end. And there, with this exquisite climate, there is all the variety of two or three civilizations; and, best of all, the presence of friends who make him feel at home.

A full fortnight after our party arrived, a fortnight which seemed much longer, so complete had been the change it wrought in all their habits; — a fortnight in which they were wonted to fruit, and roses, peas, and other summer vegetables; and, rising to a higher plane, to a climate without a touch of winter, and as yet without a breath of summer — to the real springtide of poetry — a full fortnight after their arrival they made a merry horseback party, with some officers of the garrison, and some young ladies who were now near friends; and of this party the objective was "The Springs."

The copious rush of the green waters of the San Antonio or of its sister river always makes a picturesque point whenever, in riding or in walking, you come to either stream. There is a little watering-place, perhaps under German oversight, much favored by the people who have leisure for a drive, not many miles out of the town, where, in one or another corner, is a table set in the open air — where a bridge here, a bank of willows or mesquits there, give resting-places for talk, — and where, any afternoon, there cluster throngs of children — and of grown-up children, too — who are not beyond or above being amused.

As it happened, on this particular afternoon, as the different members of the party strolled through the grounds together, Hiram Brinkerhoff and Effie Abgar stood on a great mass of rock, from beneath which pours out a stream of raging water, as the fountain of Arethusa may be supposed to rush forth from its long underground prison. No end of underground waters there. There are people who think that two-thirds of the rainfall of the Valley of the Mississippi flows in such underground currents to the sea!

Frederic Haydock and Hester Sutphen had disappeared. They were lost, as one is apt to be, on a mesquit grown prairie, and as they had often been before.

"How happy they are," said Hiram, when Mrs. Abgar had said she wondered where they would turn up this time.

"Yes indeed," was her answer; "and no one deserves happiness more than she." Her eyes flashed as she praised her friend. "You will say so, when you know her as I do. She has never sought happiness, since she gave me the biggest half of her stick of barley candy. She has never grumbled, but in fun. She has been her mother's blessing; where, indeed, any of us would have been but for her, I do not know. And, he? I hope he is as true as he seems?" This with an eager question.

"Never fear for him," said Hiram, boldly. "Truer heart never beat, under breastplate or under muslin. I am glad to see how she loves him — but she cannot love that man too well. He is as gentle as he is true, and he is as true as he is brave."

And Hiram looked as handsome as Amadis himself as he blazed up for his friend. Both of them were silent for a moment — silent from the very emotion of pride with which they had spoken — silent as well, be it added, because each was so glad to speak to somebody who could respect such enthusiasm. The man took courage first to break a silence which each enjoyed.

"I must leave this paradise to-morrow," he said, and he faltered a moment, "where I, too, have been happier than I have ever been in my life. I must go to my work again, for I too have something to do in life besides studying how I shall be happy. But I will not go till I have told you, what I think you know, how you are every thing to me; and that, in the month since I met you so happily, I have been more, seen more, known more, and hoped more than in all my life before. May I tell Amy that," and he smiled, half sadly, "and may I ask her to write to you and beg you to make me perfectly happy? There is a sweetheart who will never be jealous of you." And he smiled with that serious smile again.

No! She was not startled.

"My dear Mr. Brinkerhoff, you see in me what is not here. But I do not think that matters — I never thought I should stand where I stand — no, nor that I should say what I say. But — I should be very unwomanly — and very mean — if I did not say — as soon as I can find any words — that — that I should be very wretched, if I thought I must go back to the East alone!"

It was a blundering answer. But it served her

turn and his. He flung his arm around her and kissed her, and led her by some mysterious by-way to the gate-way of "the Springs." He found their horses, without calling on any of the rest of the party, and they rode home before the rest of the party.

Perhaps the army gentlemen thought that the New Englanders had very queer ways when they went on riding parties. If they did, they were unjust to the New Englanders; for neither Mr. Haydock the "carpet-bagger," nor Mr. Brinkerhoff the "drummer," hailed from New England.

These gentlemen made all right that evening. At Mrs. Gen. McLain's elegant party, no men were more attentive and courteous to all the guests than Mr. Haydock and his friend. Nor did the ladies lack attention, because the gentlemen of their personal escort left them mostly to the care of the gentlemen who were more at home.

As one of the groups gathered round the piano, — in illustration of some story, Lieutenant Laudonnière sang a little song in honor of Texas which he said a Spanish bishop, Don Diego Marin, wrote when Texas was yet a wilderness.

Dios te salve, tierra de Texas,
Do Natura, con hermosuras
Antes no conocidas se mostró:
    Aqui la mano divina
    Que todo lo ordena,
Con mas complacencia se paró.

El llano de tus verdes prados,
De mil colores esmaltados,
    Con la quietud del vasto mar
    Y horizonte inmenso
    Se revela estenso
Quando se ve el sol rayar.

Entre mil naranjos floridos,
Que se desmayen mis sentidos, —
Quiero mis 'lores olvidar,
    E ya no Prelado,
    E dormir sepultado
En atmosfera de Azaar.

Every one was delighted. "Only we do not understand the Spanish," said Mrs. Abgar. "'Mil colores' I can well make out, and 'naranjos,' — but then I break down."

"Then I will try again," said the Lieutenant, and he sang his little translation:

    Fair land of Texas, Heaven save thee,
    Nature her choicest blessings gave thee
And beauty all unknown before!
      The all creating Word
      Thy loveliness preferred,
Pronounced it good, and gave one blessing more!

> Enamelled plains so far extending,
> A thousand rival colors blending,
> Stretch out as broadly as the lonely sea:
> When the first sunbeams shine
> On its horizon line,
> To show how wide and lovely earth can be.
>
> Thine orange breezes gently blowing
> Sweep all away the plague of knowing,
> I lay my Bishop's grandeur gladly by,
> Beneath thy fragrant trees,
> Enjoy the scented breeze,
> And let these cares in thy Elysium die.

In the hearty applause which followed the unexpected version, our four friends looked sympathetically, each on other, as if this dear old Bishop had sung for them what they would be glad for themselves to say.

Hester broke the silence to thank the Lieutenant. "You have given Mrs. Abgar all she needed to complete her song-book."

"All? — What is that?" he asked laughing.

"Oh! Mrs. Abgar is only a Boston cockney, you know. She never dreamed of what her own country was, — one out of many. But now she has picked up, in a month's time, from the lips of her own countrymen: —

"First, a Pennsylvanian song, then a Chippeway song."

"And a German and a French," interrupted Fred Haydock.

"Don't forget the negro song, and our Texan Methodist song," said Effie.

"No! no! and there is a Norwegian song, and an Italian song, Lieutenant Laudonnière, and now you give her a Spanish song, — all sung by her own countrymen."

"Let Mrs. Abgar stay only a few weeks longer, and she shall hear a Mexican ranchero, a Camanche chief, a Greek Vivandière, and an Arab Sheikh, if I can find one of the camel drivers," said he. "They are all her countrymen, but I hope she would, all the same, be at home."

"Indeed, I should be," said Effie frankly. "And yet, do you know, Dustin, the good-natured fellow who drove our ambulance, would gladly have persuaded us to go as much farther, still in our own country, as we have come."

"Yes," said Haydock, laughing, "I overheard him. 'Just as well go on to Chihuahua, Mrs. Abgar, only five hundred miles, this team take you easy in thirty days. Just as well go on to Fort Yuma, — only six hundred miles more, — this team take you easy. And then, Mrs. Abgar, nothing to go to San Frisky. Ever been to San Frisky, Mrs. Abgar? ever been there, Miss Sutphen?' These were the words he said."

They all laughed. "But we are too much at home here," said Effie, "though now we must say good-night to Mrs. McLain."

But here came, indeed, the end of this story. Not but the ladies spent the foreordained month in San Antonio. But the gentlemen left them the morning after Gen. McLain's party, one to his office and the other to his merchandise. But when the end of May came — after Effie and Hester had had the charming month of rest and of paradise which they went for; had read and sung, and drawn and painted — had picked flowers, and pressed them and analyzed them — had talked, and slept, and dreamed to their heart's content — then their two fellow-travellers appeared again, knowing that they were ready to go back to other strawberries and to other cream.

"There is one more lion," said Mrs. Abgar to one of their hosts as he called on the last evening "which I shall ask you to take me to see. I'm sure there's a market here, — no, I don't mean a butcher's shop, a market in the open air. I always make Hester go to the markets with me. We have tried it here, but not before breakfast."

And so she had in every southwestern town where they had spent any time; and though sometimes they were not all her fancy painted, they were generally a great deal better.

Neither Hiram nor Fred knew about the San Antonio market. But Mr. La Tour said very readily that he did know; and, at half-past six in the morning of their last day, he knocked at their parlor door, and led them out of their dear Menger House, through the Alamo Plaza, and into the town beyond. "We're going to the Military Plaza," he said.

"A Plaza isn't such a mysterious thing, after all," said Hester, looking back at the gloomy beautiful Alamo, across a wide expanse of gravel and dust. "It will be a good word to astonish them with at home, but the more familiar Square describes it as well for us."

"No, indeed!" cried Effie. "Squares aren't as large."

"A Plaza was a Plaza once," said Mr. La Tour. "When you saw a little army drawn up in the Military Plaza, where we are going; or when the Greasers, as you call them, were beating through the Alamo gates behind us, — then Miss Sutphen would have found it Spanish enough."

Spanish enough they did find it, when, at the end of their walk, they came out into the great open space crowded with ox-carts, mule-carts, saddled horses, and buyers and sellers. The brown Mexicans with stiff black hair under those felt sombreros, so dear to Effie's heart, with actually leathern straps to keep them on, like little boys; light cotton shirts, red-topped boots, or leathern leggings, and an occasional crimson silk scarf round the waist, or a gay handkerchief about the neck, — such figures as these, with melancholy brown faces, as much Indian as Spanish, were quite as delightful as the ideal Texan herdsmen, though they were not at all the same thing. And the women were a new revelation of the possible beauty of the arrangement of a shawl over the head; though our travellers wished that their Moorish reserve didn't sometimes make them hold it over the lower part of the face. Such people as these they had often seen before in "San Antone," especially in Chihuahua, as they call the Mexican quarter; but never so many together, and never under such delightful circumstances. There was a little boy struggling with a lively cock which he had bought against its will; there were women selling the brightest of green and red vegetables; there — but Mr. La Tour was pointing out one group, the most Mexican of all. One of the women was sitting on the ground with a great three-legged black iron pot before her; there was no fire visible, but she was taking out and distributing some kind of hot breakfast, which her friends were eating at a table with a white cloth close by. One or two preferred squatting on the ground; her little daughter, in her gray veil, was handing round cups of coffee. Behind, were the strong light ox-carts which carry cotton to Mexico, of which some of the guests were probably drivers; farther back still, were the low, white, stucco Spanish houses of the square. Effie's sketch of part of all this was interrupted by Mr. La Tour's bringing her some of the contents of the pot: this was a little bundle, wrapped in a soft and thin corn-husk in which it had been cooked. Inside was Indian meal and red pepper and mince-meat; and, strange to say, it was very nice! It made Effie's breakfast that day.

"The meal for this must be ground by hand," said Mr. La Tour, and he led them into a pawnbroker's shop close by, where they saw low stone three-legged stools, with other stones upon them; and these, they were told, were mills, at which two women ground, almost as they did in Palestine. All sorts of other interesting things were in this shop; gay worsted hat-bands, saddles, whips, silver jewelry, every thing in fact which a Mexican can pawn to pay his gambling debts ; and unfortunately of these there are too many.

On the way home, before they crossed the pretty bridges over the deep blue river, — they thought no Swiss lake could be bluer, — on the way home, they stopped at another shop, where they could get chocolate, and graceful earthen water-coolers, and tremendous whips to carry home with them for the boys, and Mexican tobacco for the gentlemen ("the only good thing the Greasers do make" said Tom Dustin), and high colored hat-bands for Phil Abgar's boys, — and, indeed, "no end" of quaint half-savage tokens. They asked in vain for long gray silk shawls which the brown women wore; though they saw them directly afterwards in the street; their wearers were carrying great wooden cages of little birds, and offered them to the ladies with mysterious smiles. The Mexicans were almost the only women to be seen on foot in the streets. Hester had been out alone once walking; and, though no one was rude to her, she had not been sorry to rejoin her own sex: the solitude in company was as shocking as Alexander Selkirk found the tameness of the beasts. This was Spanish too.

Little appetite, after the nameless morning

cakes, for the nice Menger House breakfast. And then when the last good-byes were spoken, Dustin having been summoned once more, they started to cross the prairie to Austin. This time no brigands frightened them. They arrived just in time to secure berths "six" and "seven," "eight" and "nine," in the Pullman. Shall we say of course Aurelius was standing on the platform? — " Here's your palace car, ladies and gentlemen."

Of course the palace was the GOLCONDA.

CHAPTER XVII.

WHEN they arrived in Austin a month before, they had entered Austin in the early morning. The ladies were then alone, and rather doubtful of the adventure they were essaying; the gentlemen also were alone, a few days after, and eager to join their agreeable companions. It has been confessed already in these pages, that, of all the experiences of life in Palaces, the morning hour is the least agreeable. There is an attentive lackey, yes! But even he is engaged in making sixteen beds return to their hiding-places, and in making sixteen sofas appear in their places. There is no turbaned page with soft step to bring you a cup of coffee. There is no luxurious seat on an open veranda covered with honeysuckle and quamoclit. There is close air without, and faintness, hunger, and general misery within, till one can touch his mother earth, as Antæus did, and breathe his mother air. Then one returns to the Palace after he has breakfasted to find all changed: he is ready for empire, and another day of monarch life begins.

As all of the four whose fortunes we follow had first entered Austin from the east in such guise of the misery of early morning, it followed that there was a surprise every minute, now that they dashed eastward, caught sight of the river, and through the prairies, with the sights of beauty, which they had not guessed at when they came. Indeed — indeed — each of the four was now in a mood, than which earth has little more heavenlike; and because they were happy already, they were all the more ready to enjoy.

"May decked the world, and Arthur filled the throne."

Hester almost sang these words as they retired slowly from the open door at the rear of the car, where they had been wondering at the beauty of the cross lights and the cloud shadows on the prairie, always so marvellous.

"The last day of May," said Hiram Brinkerhoff. "But where is this line, Miss Hester, which drops from you so often, by night and morning; and is there more of the same poem? Or is it perhaps the beginning of an unpublished epic by Miss Sutphen and Mr. Haydock?

'May decked the world, and Arthur filled the throne.'"

"There is more, — and more as good as that, — if you will only search wisely, Mr. Hiram. Ask Effie there, and she will repeat to you the whole story of two happy lovers in a happy valley, — only —" and she stopped.

"Only," said Effie bravely, "that the true knight had to go away to attend to his distant duty, and the fair lady had to stay in the valley without him;" and then, more seriously, she repeated, —

> "'And I might ask how more can mortals please
>   The heavens, than thankful to enjoy the earth?
> But through its mist, my soul, though faintly, sees
>   Where thine sweeps on beyond this mountain girth,
> And awed and dazzled, bending I confess
> Life may have holier ends than happiness.'

"You see," she added after a moment, "this lady was a princess. She had always lived in palaces, and she had always done as she chose, and had had her own way, till Arthur came; and then she had to do as he chose, and let him have his own way, — even when that way took him outside the mountain valley, and far very far from her."

"All the same," said Fred, who would not come down from the extreme good-cheer of his mood, — "all the same no one tells me who this Arthur was. Was he in the wholesale drug business, travelling on account of 'Mandrake, Bromide, & Co.,' — and was this palace in which the princess lived a palace on wheels, and did he have to return to Caradoc, that the firm might be able to answer his orders for the fall trade, — or was he in the quack-nostrum line, I beg pardon, in the Panacea business, travelling for Rowland, Crespigny, & Co., — and had he heard that another house was introducing a new nervine?"

"He shall not be jeered at," said Hester reproachfully, "though he certainly was a travelling gentleman," she added. "If there are any knights of this generation who have not read Bulwer's 'King Arthur,' it is time they did. For rather staid, old-fashioned poetry, — a little machine-built, but good in doctrine, and sometimes bubbling into the supreme article — it is very good travelling reading for four wandering lovers."

"We will read it aloud between St. Louis and New York," cried Hiram. And he took a telegraph blank from the ready rack, — and, to his correspondent at St Louis, wrote, —

"Bring me Bulwer's 'King Arthur' at evening train on second."

"Tell me," said he, "that King Arthur also shall not be enthroned in the GOLCONDA."

"It is all very fine," said Hester, as he came back from forwarding his despatch, at Hempstead, — "and I am sure I like to imagine that Effie's real name is Aegle, and that mine is Elaine, but, all the same, I do not believe that Elaine or Queen Guinever herself ever had a horned frog."

"Had what?"

"Had a horned frog! Did you never see one?" And she opened her handkerchief; and gently stroked one of the weird little monsters, which, while the gentlemen were absent, she had bought of a boy at the car window.

They both affected horror at sight of the little wretch.

"He is a hundred thousand million billion years old," cried Haydock. "He was made before evolution began. The evening and the morning were the first day."

"Aegle was stroking him when Arthur bade her good-by in the happy valley," said Hiram. "He carries you back behind all the Babels."

"Some merits he has which later times have lost," said Hester, "for he needs no food, and I believe no water.

'With temperance he both eats and drinks,
  And gives the poor the whole.'"

"He is no more a frog than I am," cried Effie,

with her naturalist skill. "He is a lizard of the genus *Phrynosoma*, whatever that may mean. He is *Phrynosoma orbiculare*, because, if you please, his body is so orbicular. And dear old Phil will be glad to have him to catch flies in the green-house, and to amuse the boys: they have all seen him in the Iconographic Cyclopædia. I am not sure but he is *cornuta* and not *orbiculare*."

"Do you say he eats nothing?"

"Oh, not for a week or two, if his keepers are on their last greenbacks, as we are."

"He looks as if he had eaten nothing since

    'This fair world first rounded to the view.'

You will never tell me that Texas is a new country again."

"Can anybody tell me," said Effie, as the train moved away from the station, and they began their northward way, — "why Texas was left out till the very end of time. When such crags and deserts as those of Tommy's rocks in Roxbury, and the marshes of Cambridgeport have been peopled, — why has this lovely Texas with these

    'Enamelled plains so far extending,'

been left desert, and without any people but these ante-creationals."

"Philip the Second, my dear," said Hester. "Fred has been coaching me."

"Pope Alexander the Sixth," said Fred. "Hiram has been lecturing to me."

"Laziness and greed," said Brinkerhoff: "there was never such a horrible illustration of bad government."

"Poor La Salle," he continued, "after he had discovered the course of the Mississippi, came out here with a colony, — and here they killed him: he must have crossed our line, I fancy, not so very far from where we are."

"That gave France a right here, if there were any right; and that made Spain afraid that France would come near her silver mines yonder. And so, as Hester says, Spain enacted that neither oil-olive, nor luscious grape, neither wheat nor maize, nor sugar nor cotton, should grow on these thousands upon thousands of thousands of acres. Better they should lie waste for ever, than that the most Catholic King's people and the most Christian King's people should come too near together."

"What broke all that down?"

"To answer in very short metre, — Philip Nolan broke it down, so Judge Harford here says. If I could make you stop two days longer, we would go over to Waco yonder, and find his grave, and plant lilies upon it."

"And I might liberate my frog there."

But there was not much more talk. A sharp thunder-storm struck them as it grew dark, and there was little for it, but to look at this fork of the "flames of the lightning," and to wonder at that crash, till Aurelius changed the day palace into a night palace.

And when they woke again, they were crossing the Red River, more than two hundred miles higher up than they had left it at Shreveport. And how red it is! almost vermilion! And this country, too, "the garden of Texas" as they were assured, was laughing with beauty.

And then, not long after, they bade Texas good-by. And now they were in the Indian Territory. And all that day — stopping not once an hour — they were speeding north, with this same eager flight, through the rich green of the prairie land, of wealth which cannot be told; and for an hour at a time there would be no sign of man but the track of the railway!

"Oh dear, oh dear!" sighed Effie, "if my poor Shays, and Donavans and Mrs. Murphy and the Holden boys were only here, instead of starving in Lucas Street and in Oswego Street, instead of drinking in Sands Court, and dying of cholera infantum in Swett Street."

"Do you know why they are not here, and why they cannot be here? Do you know why Rothschild, with all his wealth, cannot buy an acre of this land?" This was Hiram's question.

"Cannot! I thought money could do every thing. It could at Fort Sill yonder," and Hester pointed over her shoulder westward.

"Cannot," said Fred Haydock, laughing, "unless Baron Rothschild married a Cherokee lady! Then he might buy till he were tired, — or, indeed, have, without buying, I believe."

Then Hiram explained that the United States government had bound itself by treaty with the Cherokees and Chickasaws and Choctaws, and Creeks and Seminoles and Muscogees, — never to sell any of this land, as long as the winds should blow or the waters flow. He explained that, all told, there were not a hundred thousand of these Indians. But that, such is the force of treaties, these hundred thousand Indians, who are not hunters, generally speaking, but have settled down to farming, have a matchless territory, a third part the size of France, given to them; which is, acre for acre, far more productive than France is. He explained that no one, not an Indian of another tribe even, might enter here, because the United States had made these treaties with these people.

"Will any one explain to me," said Effie, "in what this policy differs from that of Philip the Second?"

But nobody explained.

All the same, the train dashed on. There is something almost weird and uncanny in this sailing through oceans of green, only broken by pretty copses of wood or gentle swells of land, without a fence, a house, a barn, a road beside that you travel on, without cow or horse or sheep. Only an unused fertile world waiting for men!

But at every station-house, there would be one or two men waiting, and sometimes a passenger. They must have come from somewhere. And once there was a college, after they came into the Cherokee country. But Hester confesses that, in her journal, it is not the political economy that is noted, nor the advance of the Cherokees in education, but that good supper at Muskogee!

On and on! Conundrums as it grew dark in the evening; an effort to talk with the reticent half-breed lady who came into the car on her way northward, where she had a daughter at school in Ohio. And then, all the light melts away, though we are in June; and, as they begin to be drowsy, even the substantial fabric of the palace melts away, the sofas are gone, the people are gone, and "Six and Seven" have been "made up" by the faithful Aurelius, and the tired travellers "turn in."

Asleep and unconscious they pass through Kansas, where in old times their own brothers had fought and conquered. They wake to another climate, and another vegetation. They are in the South no longer. They are in a desert no longer. They are forging on and on, down the valleys that lead to the Missouri, with here a town and there a town, and all the first scars of man's conflict with nature.

What seems strangest of all, in such a journey, is the setting back of the orchards and farmlands some three weeks, between your night and your morning. When you pass in a day a beautiful desert like the Indian Territory, so as to leave, as these people had done, the gardens of northern Texas on Tuesday morning to come into those of central Missouri on Wednesday morning, with no fine gradation by the way, but by one sudden leap, it is all the more strange.

They had a Sunday-school picnic tumbled in on the train somewhere, a strawberry party or some such entertainment. And when, at Jefferson, Hiram rushed out to forage, he was led away by the throng. For he acted on Jacob Abbot's direction to Rollo, for travelling, " Go where the rest go." But, as he soon found that, if he went to hear the Rev. Abner Goosh make a "few remarks" to the children, he should not rejoin his own party, he was seen by them rushing wildly back to the station-house, only in time to seize from a licensed dealer a loaf of bread, to wave it in the air over the head of a deacon, so as to attract the licensed dealer's attention, and to deposit, as probable pay, two nickels on the counter. Even with these abridgments of the process of bargaining, Hiram returned to the GOLCONDA only as she began to move.

"It was," he said, "as Miles Standish took the corn, and left in its place a leather jerkin, though he saw no salvages."

So this large loaf was to be their lunch, for they had voted not to dine till they came to St. Louis. Then was it that the innate hospitality appeared, of those who live in Palaces. The Russian gentleman from Alaska, who had come in, in the night, offered caviare, the Mexican gentleman, who had been a fellow passenger all the way from Austin, offered chocolate, the half-breed lady offered butter, which was of all the sweeter taste, because it was Cherokee butter from a Cherokee cow. Knives, forks, spoons, vodka if they would have had it, nay, probably, saki from Japan. So our friends made a merry picnic, from a table served by half the world.

"Do you remember in the 'Evenings at Home' a Presbyterian offered her smelling-bottle, and a Quaker ran for the doctor?"

"Do I remember it? It comes down like a forgotten prophecy of the kingdom coming! But I can see now the broad-brimmed man, in the picture. The only time, I think that I ever saw a Quaker run, always excepting Obed Macy when we played foot-ball in college."

And now they were by the Southern side of the Missouri. The great "rampage" was not over, on which they had all four floated, two months before.

"Since we met, I have been reading La Salle's account of this very 'Muddy' River, Pekatonoui they called it, which meant muddy."

"Men change, but rivers do not. But think, — I suppose he was half a year coming here from Canada, and when shall we cross the Niagara?"

"Before we wake on Thursday morning!"

"That is flying, indeed!"

And at St. Louis the faithful and hospitable Jabez Cottingham appeared, with the needed "King Arthur." Surely they would stop for a few days. No! not they. They were homeward bound, and they could only stop for the supper, which was their dinner, and then on again in the GOLCONDA. For the good fortune of this particular visit had ordered her back to New York again.

So they crossed, as day paled, the wonderful bridge; but of Illinois they can tell little, for they slept as they swept through.

"Illinois," said Hiram, "means 'men.' The natives here would not acknowledge that there were any others." And, when they breakfasted in that weird, many-landish breakfast-room at Chicago, he told where that word "Chicago" appears first in literature. It was at a great council which Tonti held in 1659, when chiefs from Chicago were made to give in their fealty to Le Grand Monarque, Louis XIV. Does some Chicago King of Corn and Corners think of that some day, as he walks through the battle gallery of republican Versailles?

On and on, for ever on! We oil the wheels. We feed the men and women. We water the engine. But that is all, and we rush through Michigan for another day.

"Si peninsulam amoenam quaeris, circumspice." This is the droll motto of the State. Droll but very true! Names all mixed together, from all the eras of history, — Niles, Kalamazoo, Homer, Jackson, Ann Arbor, Ypsilanti, and Detroit! A well-read man he, profound in the philosophy of history, who will weave together, in the damask web of a day's story, the threads which are spun out by the associations of those names! And at Detroit, such a sunset! and such a supper! It is your last of Western profusion, Hester and Effie, Hiram and Fred!

Night drops a curtain over Canada, but still we rush on! Yes, we do not even wake to see Niagara in the morning. We do not really wake till we breakfast at Rochester!

And all that day, as our little party were whirled on in their palace over that New York Central Road, which Mr. Howells has made classical for lovers and for travellers, they had to wonder at the agriculture of the North, as if they had come from another world. Two cows only together, or at most ten or twelve! How lonely they must be! and how small these fields! how narrow all these measures, to people who had forgotten fences, and felt as if all men owned, if they would take it, all the world!

And if they felt this in New York, how much more when they came to the gardens — farms no longer — of their dear Massachusetts! But how delicious home was! How they rushed from window to window to see a mountain or cascade! How they sympathized with the little boy from Illinois, when he called his mother to show to her the marvel, which he saw for the first time, — a Yankee "stone wall"!

On and on! Night settled on them at Palmer. Still it was on and on! And when, at last, they swept into the sight of Charles River by the Arsenal in Watertown, as it lay there beautiful under the moon so nearly full, the Tenore Assoluto of the party sang the last song of the Palace Journey.

At Springfield they had lost most of their companions, with eager goodbyes and promises of mutual visits. At Worcester, that nice Australian lady, with her five boys, who had come through from San Francisco by palace, left them that she might go on to Halifax, by the route which leaves Boston out in the cold. So was it that our friends were all alone between Worcester and Boston. For the GOLCONDA did not regularly belong on that line, nor do I know how it came there.

As they swept by the Arsenal at Watertown, and the moon shone brightly on the river, Hiram broke out, as of old on the Juniata, into singing: —

I sang in the daylight, I sing in the dark,
I sing by Charles River, I sang by San Marc;

I sang in the mesquit, until the woods rang —
By the blue Juniata I rode and I sang.

From the land of the olive, the orange, and vine,
The mesquit sent love to the cedar and pine.

The land of the jasmine, the myrtle, and rose,
Has sent my true love to the land of the snows.

The land of the sunset that's glowing afar,
Has sent my true love to the cold northern star.

But at this moment all romance ceased. A belated baggage agent came into the palace for orders. "Baggage taken to any part of the city. What hotel, Sir?"

And the glamour of the orange and vine left them; and, as they saw the gas lights of the Western Avenue and Beacon Street, they knew that the journey of the dear GOLCONDA was ended.

"Dear, dear Philip! and are the children all well?"

"Well and hearty, — and you?"

"All well! we are all well! This is Hiram — I mean this is Mr. Brinkerhoff, and this is Mr. Haydock."

And Philip had kissed Hester Sutphen already.

THE END.

Cambridge: Press of John Wilson & Son.

TOWN AND COUNTRY SERIES.

A WINTER STORY.

By MISS PEARD,

AUTHOR OF "THE ROSE GARDEN," "UNAWARES," "THORPE REGIS."

"The author of 'The Rose Garden' has written a fresh novel, which Roberts Brothers have just published in their 'Town and Country Series,' under the title 'A Winter Story.' The volumes of this series are well printed, tastefully bound in cloth, with appropriate designs stamped on the cover, and are sold at a dollar each."

"Another volume of the 'Town and Country Series' contains the latest of Miss Peard's pretty novelettes. 'A Winter Story' is extremely simple and unaffected in style, and possesses the same quiet charm that characterized 'The Rose Garden' and 'Unawares.' Whoever has read the former will seek to know what this pleasing writer has to say, in her idyllic way, about love and other kindred matters, in the present volume. The scene is laid in an English village, but deals with uncommon people in very peculiar circumstances."

"We confess to a liking for this 'Winter Story' of hers which possesses a good deal of originality and ingenuity. It is a thoughtful tale, with a good deal more in it than appears at first sight on the surface. It is a story which actually grows in favor with the reader, and the interest is well kept up. Miss Peard is making strides in her profession, and each new novel is better than her last. We can commend this latest edition of the 'Town and Country Series' to lovers of a healthy tone of fiction."

Our publications are to be had of all booksellers. When not to be found, send directly to

ROBERTS BROTHERS, *Publishers*,

BOSTON.

PUBLISHERS' ADVERTISEMENT.

From the Boston Daily Advertiser.

THE "NO NAME SERIES."

"LEIGH HUNT, *in his 'Indicator,' has a pleasant chapter on the difficulty he encountered in seeking a suitable and fresh title for a collection of his miscellaneous writings. Messrs. Roberts Brothers have just overcome a similar difficulty in the simplest manner. In selecting* "NO NAME," *they have selected the very best title possible for a series of Original American Novels and Tales, to be published Anonymously. These novels are to be written by eminent authors, and in each case the authorship of the work is to remain an inviolable secret.* "*No Name*" *describes the Series perfectly. No name will help the novel, or the story, to success. Its success will depend solely on the writer's ability to catch and retain the reader's interest. Several of the most distinguished writers of American fiction have agreed to contribute to the Series, the initial volume of which is now in press. Its appearance will certainly be awaited with curiosity.*"

The plan thus happily foreshadowed will be immediately inaugurated by the publication of "MERCY PHILBRICK'S CHOICE," from the pen of a well-known and successful writer of fiction.

It is intended to include in the Series a volume of anonymous poems from famous hands, to be written especially for it.

The "No Name Series" will be issued at convenient intervals, in handsome library form, 16mo, cloth, price $1.00 each.

ROBERTS BROTHERS, PUBLISHERS.

BOSTON, Midsummer, 1876.

www.ingramcontent.com/pod-product-compliance
Lightning Source LLC
Chambersburg PA
CBHW021806230426
43669CB00008B/653